Teaching the Word

Religious Education at Brigham Young University

Richard O. Cowan

RELIGIOUS STUDIES CENTER
BRIGHAM YOUNG UNIVERSITY

RELIGIOUS STUDIES CENTER
BRIGHAM YOUNG UNIVERSITY

Published by the Religious Studies Center, Brigham Young University, Provo, Utah
http://religion.byu.edu/rsc_rec_pub.php

ISBN 978-0-8425-2708-8

Joseph Smith Building cover photo courtesy of Richard B. Crookston
Sacred Grove background photo courtesy of Brent R. Nordgren

Contents

Preface

I first wrote a history of Religious Education at Brigham Young University during the 1970s in preparation for publication of the university's centennial history. This present brief history was written during the 1990s in response to an assignment from Dean Robert L. Millet and is now being updated at the request of Dean Terry B. Ball. I have appreciated the encouragement and assistance of these leaders as this project has moved forward. I am also grateful to Patty Smith, who has compiled several large scrapbooks containing a variety of clippings, photographs, programs, minutes, and other documents that have been valuable sources of information. Richard D. Draper, former associate dean of Religious Education, worked with me in this update, and I particularly appreciate his helpful effort.

Kent P. Jackson (associate dean) suggested to Richard Neitzel Holzapfel (publications director, RSC) that this short history could be enhanced by the inclusion of many more images and additional subject matter and published as a hardback edition. The story deserves this special attention. I therefore appreciate the RSC for making this happen, including R. Devan Jensen (editor), Nathan E. Richardson and Kristin McGuire (designers), and Stephanie H. Wilson and Brent R. Nordgren (production managers).

Having joined the faculty in 1961, I have personally experienced many of the events described here. The opportunity to have taught the gospel to thousands of students for nearly half a century and to have associated with outstanding colleagues has been a rare privilege. I hope that this history adequately reflects the important individuals, decisions, and developments shaping Religious Education's present status, mission, and accomplishments and that reading this work will help you more fully understand and appreciate our role in the university and in the Church.

Richard O. Cowan

Beginnings

1875–1959

Religious Education faculty and staff members identify with those whose commission it was in ancient times "to teach the word of God among all the people" (Helaman 5:14; see also Alma 23:4; 38:15; 2 Timothy 4:2). Therefore, it has been their desire, as it was with two of Lehi's sons, to "teach . . . the word of God with all diligence" (Jacob 1:19). Religious instruction has been a central part of Brigham Young University's unique mission since the beginning.

Brigham Young's Charge

President Brigham Young, founder of the university that bears his name, believed that all branches of education were important but that religious instruction needed extra emphasis. In 1852 he declared, "There are a great many branches of education. . . . But our favourite study is that branch which particularly belongs to the Elders of Israel—namely, theology. Every Elder should become a profound theologian— should understand this branch better than all the world."[1]

Specifically, Brigham Young Academy's 1875 deed of trust directed that "all pupils shall be instructed in reading, penmanship, orthography, grammar, geography, and mathematics, together with such other branches as are usually taught in an academy of learning; and the Old and New Testaments, the Book of Mormon and the Book of Doctrine and Covenants shall be read and their doctrines inculcated in the Academy."[2]

Statue of Karl G. Maeser, by Ortho R. Fairbanks. The first permanent principal of Brigham Young Academy, Karl G. Maeser was taught by Brigham Young that spiritual development is an inseparable part of higher education. Courtesy of Richard B. Crookston.

The next year, when Karl G. Maeser was sent to Provo to head the school, President Young instructed him: "Brother Maeser, I want you to remember that you ought not to teach even the alphabet or the multi-

---

1. Brigham Young, in *Journal of Discourses* (London: Latter-day Saints' Book Depot, 1854–86), 6:317.
2. Deed of Trust, quoted in John P. Fugal, "University-wide Religious Objectives: Their History and Implementation at Brigham Young University" (PhD diss., Brigham Young University, 1967), 36.

plication tables, without the spirit of God. That is all. God bless you. Good-bye."[3]

The influence of President Young's philosophy has continued as a vital force in the twentieth century. In 1940 the Church Board of Education declared that its educational institutions and activities were maintained for three major reasons. First was "to provide the youth of Zion with religious training such as cannot be obtained in public schools; to teach the doctrines of the Church of Jesus Christ of Latter-day Saints; to help establish within the students the testimony of the truth of the divine work established through the instrumentality of Joseph Smith, the Prophet; and thus to fit them for useful life in the Church, as intelligent, faithful, active Latter-day Saints."[4]

Consistent with this direction, BYU's 1981 mission statement affirmed that the university was to "assist individuals in their quest for perfection and eternal life." Similarly, "spiritually strengthening" was listed as the first among the "Aims of a BYU Education," adopted in 1995.

Early Religious Curriculum

From the beginning, the religious character of the curriculum was apparent. In 1879, James E. Talmage, who that year became a teacher at the academy, one month before his seventeenth birthday, reminded his class: "All our conduct in this academy, of teachers as well as students, all

---

3. Reinhard Maeser, *Karl G. Maeser: A Biography by His Son* (Provo, UT: Brigham Young University, 1928), 79, as quoted in Fugal, "Religious Objectives," 36.

4. Quoted in Fugal, "Religious Objectives," 26.

our discipline, all our studies are conducted according to the spirit of the living God."[5]

During the 1880s, there were daily religion classes and devotionals. Furthermore, President John Taylor affirmed, all other subjects were to be taught in such a way that faith in the gospel would not be undermined. "It is this feature of teaching the principles of our religion, and embodying all other studies in them, which constitute one of the chief excellencies of the system of education at the B.Y. Academy."[6]

During the early years of the twentieth century, however, there was increasing tension between traditional beliefs and new scientific ideas. Unfortunately, an investigation in 1911 found that three BYU faculty members employed the "higher criticism" of the Bible and questioned the historicity of certain events of the Restoration. As a result, the Board of Trustees recommended their dismissal. In the wake of this divisive controversy, President Joseph F. Smith advised against teaching any concepts that could be misleading or undermine faith.[7]

The 1912–13 catalog emphasized that the courses in theology were based on the standard works, the aim being to give the students a "theoretical understanding," as well as practical application, of gospel principles in the light of latter-day revelation "in order that students may have faith in God and develop a religious character." The curriculum consisted of

---

5. "Theological References," October 13, 1879, book 2, p. 9; University Archives.
6. Letter to stake presidents and bishops, *Inquirer*, June 10, 1887.
7. Ernest L. Wilkinson and W. Cleon Skousen, *Brigham Young University: A School of Destiny* (Provo, UT: Brigham Young University Press, 1976), 200–212.

Brigham Young Academy student body, 1902–3. Between 1892 and 1903, the student body more than quadrupled, growing from 275 to 1,622. The blessings of an education intertwined with the doctrines of the Restoration were being made available to more and more people (see Ernest L. Wilkinson, "Highlights in the Ninety-Nine-Year History of BYU," October 10, 1974, speeches.byu.edu). Courtesy of University Archives, L. Tom Perry Special Collections, Harold B. Lee Library, BYU.

yearlong courses, each meeting four times a week, in Book of Mormon, New Testament, Old Testament, and Church history and doctrine.[8]

A decade later, the "theology" offering was expanded and substantially changed because the basic questions facing the youth were not the same as in former generations. Most of the fifty-one listed courses were in the Bible, philosophy, Christian and other world religions, and even such related areas as teaching children, hymnology, Scouting, public speaking,

---

8. *Annual Catalogue*, 1912–13, 82.

and recreational and dance leadership. There was only one course each in such uniquely Latter-day Saint subjects as the Book of Mormon, Church history, and Mormon theology, even though these courses were the most appealing to students.[9]

The Brigham Young Academy building, Provo, Utah. Designed by Don Carlos Young, son of Brigham Young, and built of brick and sandstone, the building housed Brigham Young Academy and Brigham Young High School until it was closed in 1968. It stood empty for over thirty years, when various donors raised several million dollars to renovate and modernize it. It now serves as the Provo City Library at Academy Square, continuing to provide educational opportunities to the community through various programs. Courtesy of University Archives, L. Tom Perry Special Collections, Harold B. Lee Library, BYU.

9. Ernest L. Wilkinson, ed., *Brigham Young University: The First One Hundred Years* (Provo, UT: Brigham Young University Press, 1965), 2:289–90.

A religion major was offered from 1927 to 1935. Students who wished to prepare for working with children, youth, or adults in the auxiliary organizations of the Church were permitted to major in theology, supplementing the regular courses in that department with additional classes in education and psychology.[10]

Graduate Program Initiated

The first graduate program of any kind at BYU began in 1916, and graduate offerings in religious education came six years later in 1922. At first, graduate religion courses were offered by various colleges on campus, but they were not taught by regular faculty members and were held only during the summer. In 1922, for example, the Education Department brought Dr. Charles Edward Rugh from the University of California to teach classes on religious education and the Bible.

The 1927 program was more directly aimed at seminary principals and teachers. Elder John A. Widtsoe, a member of the Quorum of the Twelve and former president of the University of Utah, offered a course in "Current Problems," including the "higher criticism" of the Bible and the relationship between science and religion. Adam S. Bennion, superintendent of Church schools, also offered a course in the social and ethical aspects of religion.[11]

In 1929 Joseph F. Merrill (who became a member of the Twelve two years later) became the Church commissioner of education. He was convinced that "men of strong spirituality" as well as "good scholarship" were

---

10. *Annual Catalogue*, 1927–28, 187; see corresponding entries in the following eight issues.
11. Wilkinson, *The First One Hundred Years*, 2:287.

needed in the Church's seminaries and institutes; therefore, he organized a special religion offering during the BYU summer session in 1929. He called Sidney B. Sperry, a doctoral student in Old Testament languages and literature at the University of Chicago and former seminary teacher, to give two courses in Old Testament.[12] Merrill then asked Sperry to recommend other scholars who might be invited to come in succeeding years. During the next four summers, classes were presented on the BYU campus by world-class scholars from the University of Chicago, such as New Testament translator Edgar J. Goodspeed and Christian history professor John T. McNeill.[13] "But there was a limit to what they could contribute," noted Elder Boyd K. Packer of the Quorum of the Twelve, because they lacked the priesthood and inspiration of the Spirit.[14]

Beginning in 1929, graduate classes in "religious education" (which that year replaced the designation "theology"), were offered during the regular school year. The first students to receive master of science degrees with majors in religious education graduated in 1930. This honor went to Victor C. Anderson and H. Alvah Fitzgerald; the latter returned a quarter of a century later as a faculty member in the College of Religious Instruction.[15]

12. Sidney B. Sperry, "History of a Graduate Religion at BYU," unpublished paper delivered November 15, 1969, 3.

13. Sperry, "Graduate Religion," 3–4.

14. Boyd K. Packer, "Seek Learning Even by Study and Also by Faith," in *Religious Education Foundational Readings* (n.p.: Religious Education, Brigham Young University, June 2005), 28.

15. *54th Annual Commencement of the Brigham Young University*, June 4, 1930.

Guy C. Wilson, first full-time religion teacher at BYU, 1930–41. Wilson's many previous teaching jobs and Church assignments prepared him to play a pioneering role in the genesis of religious education at BYU. Courtesy of University Archives, L. Tom Perry Special Collections, Harold B. Lee Library, BYU.

A Distinct Religion Faculty

From the beginning until 1930, religion classes were taught entirely by BYU faculty members who accepted this assignment in addition to work in their own disciplines. The expansion of the religion curriculum, and especially the introduction of graduate courses during the 1920s, made a change in this pattern advisable. Hence, the first full-time religion teacher at BYU, Guy C. Wilson, began his work on the campus in 1930. Even though others, including Joseph B. Keeler and George H. Brimhall, had the title professor of theology, a review of their teaching load and other university assignments indicates they were not full-time teachers of religion.

Guy C. Wilson earned the bachelor of pedagogy degree from the Brigham Young Academy in 1902 and then pursued graduate studies at four schools, including the University of Chicago and Columbia University. After serving fifteen years as principal of the Juárez Academy in northern Mexico, Wilson organized the Church's first seminary at Granite High School in Salt Lake City in 1912. He later presided over the Latter-day

Saints University (also in Salt Lake City) and from 1926 to 1930 served as the supervisor of religious education for the Church Department of Education. It was from this last assignment that he came to BYU as a professor of religious education until his retirement in 1941.

To meet the need for qualified teachers of religion, Commissioner Merrill encouraged a number of promising young seminary and institute teachers to go east for advanced training. Unfortunately, lamented Elder Packer years later, "some who went never returned. And some of them who returned never came back. They had followed, they supposed, the scriptural injunction: 'Seek learning, even by study and also by faith' (Doctrine and Covenants 88:118). But somehow the mix had been wrong, for they had sought learning out of the best books, even by study, but with too little faith."[16] One who both received advanced training and came back was Sidney B. Sperry, who joined the faculty on a permanent basis in 1932.

The Division of Religion

Although BYU catalogs from as early as 1902 listed religion classes under the heading "Department of Theology," there was no official organization until 1940. In January of that year, the Board of Trustees organized the "Division of Religion" under the immediate direction of the president of the university. It was to have "co-ordinate academic standing with the schools of the University" and was to be "a general service division to all university departments in the field of religious education." In addition to supervising "religious instruction," the division was also

---

16. Packer, "Seek Learning," 28.

responsible for "all religious activities on campus," including devotionals, Sunday School, and the Mutual Improvement Association.

Students were required to take six quarter hours of religion each year, and the division issued certificates to those who completed thirty-six hours of religion as was being done in the institutes. Actual degrees in religion were offered only on the graduate level.[17]

J. Wyley Sessions, who had joined the faculty as director of religious activities in 1939, assumed leadership in the new division. While working on a master's degree at the University of Idaho, he organized the Church's first "Institute of Religion" there in 1926.[18] He supervised the construction of an attractive building which would meet the students' social as well as spiritual needs. He later served as Institute director in Pocatello, Idaho;

J. Wyley Sessions, director of religious activities, 1939–47. Sessions sought to unify the scattered endeavors of the religion professors while still keeping religious education tied to and supported by the other colleges on campus. He also took part in designing the original Joseph Smith Building. Courtesy of University Archives, L. Tom Perry Special Collections, Harold B. Lee Library, BYU.

Laramie, Wyoming; and Logan, Utah, traveling widely as a consultant for similar programs and buildings at other western campuses.

17. Executive Committee of the BYU Board of Trustees, minutes, January 5, 1940.
18. A. Gary Anderson, "A Historical Survey of the Full-time Institutes of Religion" (PhD diss., Brigham Young University, 1968), 44.

When he came to BYU, Sessions found teachers of religion scattered all over campus. Without central direction, the professors taught as they pleased. His goal was to form a curriculum that would provide the strongest possible religion program. He did not see the teaching of religion as being "set off or apart" but believed the Division of Religion should be "tied to, affiliated with, and supported by all the colleges of the University."[19] Within the division, there were four subject-area departments, each headed by a chairman.

Division of Religion
1940

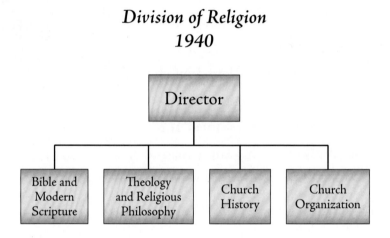

The Joseph Smith Building

As religious activities and instruction expanded, the need for an adequate facility to house them became increasingly apparent. BYU president Franklin S. Harris, for example, lamented that only one-third of the student body could be accommodated in College Hall on lower

---

19. J. Wyley Sessions interview, June 29, 1965.

The original Joseph Smith Building. Designed by Fred L. Markham, the building stood for fifty years, from 1941 to 1991. Its replacement was designed by his two sons, John and Dix (see page 61). Courtesy of L. Tom Perry Special Collections, Harold B. Lee Library, BYU.

campus where the regular devotional assemblies were held: "Thus the majority were denied much of the very things that make Brigham Young University unique. Students coming from far away primarily to secure the spiritual advantages of the Institution were able to obtain these advantages only in part."[20] The General Authorities were particularly concerned with the students' spiritual welfare. President Heber J. Grant, for example, felt that the next building built on the campus should be a

---

20. *Souvenir of the Dedication of the Joseph Smith Building, Brigham Young University Quarterly* 38 (November 1, 1941): 1.

Joseph Smith Building groundbreaking, fall 1939. Courtesy of L. Tom Perry Special Collections, Harold B. Lee Library, BYU.

chapel and that no other construction should take place there until the religious character of the school was well established.[21]

Church commissioner of education Franklin L. West had assigned J. Wyley Sessions, who was still consulting on new institute buildings, to design an institute building to serve thirty-five hundred to four thousand students. Sessions did not know where the large new institute building was to be built but thought it was for the University of Utah; it was not until he came to BYU in 1939 that he learned the structure would be for BYU.[22] Fred L. Markham of Provo was appointed architect, and a faculty committee supervised the project. Construction began in the fall of 1939 on what would become the original Joseph Smith Building.

The General Authorities decided to make the construction of this building a Church welfare project. The bishops in the twelve cooperating stakes were responsible for procuring the required workmen. When this supply of labor from the wards was insufficient, BYU students stepped in to help, contributing many days. On "Y Day" in 1941, all the male stu-

---

21. Fred L. Markham, interview by M. Ephraim Hatch, November 1, 1973, in "History of the Brigham Young University Campus and Department of Physical Plant," manuscript, 4:25, University Archives.

22. Sessions interview.

The Joseph Smith Building portrayed in the BYU yearbook The Banyan, *1948, pages 40–41. An artist superimposed an image of a stairway into the sky over a photo of the Joseph Smith Building to depict the importance of the Spirit in educational achievement. Courtesy of L. Tom Perry Special Collections, Harold B. Lee Library, BYU.*

dents participated in constructing the walks around the building. Provo businesses contributed three thousand dollars. Funds from a special fast day were used to buy produce to pay the workers.[23]

The building was dedicated on Founders' Day, October 16, 1941. President Harris reminded the assembled congregation of the sacrifices made by the many individuals who had assisted in the construction and given "thousands of voluntary days of work."[24] President David O. McKay, Second Counselor in the First Presidency, affirmed that "it is fitting that there should be on this campus an edifice bearing the name

---

23. *Souvenir,* 5.
24. *Founders' Day Report,* October 16, 1941, manuscript, University Archives.

The Joseph Smith Building, dedicated in 1941. Courtesy of L. Tom Perry Special Collections, Harold B. Lee Library, BYU.

of the Prophet Joseph Smith. . . . Without revelation given to Joseph Smith there would be no Brigham Young University. In all classes here at this school there should be connoted [the] great truth: that God lives, that Jesus is the Christ, and that Joseph Smith was the divinely inspired Prophet of the Lord, chosen to establish Christ's Church on earth in this latter day." He described the new edifice as "a place of worship, a temple of learning, and a place of spiritual communion," which stood for the "complete education of youth—the truest and the best in life."[25]

At the time of the new building's dedication, university officials anticipated that it would have a significant impact on the school's programs: "The need of this building and the contributions it will make to the future of Brigham Young University and to the entire Church cannot be over-estimated."[26]

---

25. *Founders' Day Report*, October 16, 1941.
26. *Souvenir*, 6–7.

The auditorium in the original Joseph Smith Building. Notice the compromised theater but pewlike seating to accommodate both religious and social events. Courtesy of L. Tom Perry Special Collections, Harold B. Lee Library, BYU.

In addition to providing the badly needed auditorium and classrooms, the new Joseph Smith Building included other facilities that accommodated a variety of campus activities. Behind the auditorium was a large, beautiful ballroom that doubled as an overflow area. The campus's main cafeteria was located in the basement of the building's south wing. A "banquet hall" occupied the building's southeast corner. A special meal service was also offered in the adjoining "Club Room" at noon for members of the faculty and others—a precursor to the service later offered in the Sky Room. Beginning in 1952, major dramatic productions, including many of Shakespeare's plays, were presented on the JSB auditorium's stage.

Postwar Growth

From 1939 until his retirement in 1947, Sessions served as director of Religious Activity, and Hugh B. Brown served briefly in the same office. In 1949 the office was discontinued because responsibility for social and related activities had been shifted from the Division of Religion to the recently created Church branches on campus (these branches would be organized into the first BYU stake on January 8, 1956). In

Sidney B. Sperry, director of Religious Instruction, 1947–53. Sperry strongly held that the quality of religious instruction was enhanced by high-quality scholarship. He thus encouraged advanced degrees, particularly in areas such as languages. His influence was such that the annual Sidney B. Sperry Symposium was named for him (see pages 43–45, 53). Courtesy of University Archives, L. Tom Perry Special Collections, Harold B. Lee Library, BYU.

1947 Sidney B. Sperry was called to fill a new post, director of Religious *Instruction*, clearly in charge of only academic work.

Even though Sperry received his bachelor's degree in chemistry and began teaching high school math and science, in 1922 he made the decision to become a seminary teacher. Following his doctoral training as one of the young men who went east for graduate education, in 1932 he became BYU's second full-time religion teacher. Sperry's contributions were not limited to the BYU campus. His pioneering lecture series in Utah, Idaho, Nevada, California, Washington, and Alberta anticipated the far-flung "Education Week" and Know Your Religion lectures of later years. His dozen books and countless articles also served to spread his influence. He even had the distinction of leading the first BYU Travel Study tour in the Holy Land in 1953.

As Dr. Sperry assumed his role as director of Religious Instruction, he had "great hopes for the Division of Religion; he had the desire and vision that some day it would become spiritually and scholastically the greatest in the world."[27] To this end Sperry sought teachers who had both a thorough command of their subjects and a firm testimony of the gospel. Under Dr. Sperry's leadership, the religion faculty experienced a dramatic increase from only four in 1947 to twenty-nine a decade later. Following the example of Commissioner Merrill twenty years earlier, Dr. Sperry encouraged promising potential teachers to seek further training in the leading universities of the country. David H. Yarn, a future dean of religion, paid tribute to Sperry's leadership and personal example and affirmed that "to him more than any other person goes credit for the confidence the Brethren have established in this college for both individual and collective effort in preparation of manuals, handbooks, teacher supplements, etc."[28]

The religion curriculum also felt the impact of Dr. Sperry's influence. Under his direction, the number of undergraduate courses in the modern scriptures increased from three to ten. Similarly, by 1958, graduate courses expanded from six to ninety-two, including forty-two in languages. The Bible courses increased from one to twenty-one during this period, and where there had been no graduate courses on Latter-day Saint scriptures or Church history in 1938, the offerings in these areas reached six and ten classes, respectively.

As early as 1929 the catalog had referred to a master's degree with a major in religious education. In 1958 the Division of Religion began offering the PhD in scripture and Church history and also launched the new master of religious education (MRE) degree. Five years later the

---

27. Sperry, "A Graduate Religion," 10.
28. Yarn, "A Tribute to Sperry," 3–4.

doctor of religious education (DRE) degree was added. Unlike the PhD, the DRE was a "service degree" designed especially to meet the needs of seminary and institute teachers.[29] In 1963, Melvin S. Tagg was the first to earn a PhD in religion.[30] Over the years more than two hundred theses and dissertations were written on religious topics. "There is a definite need in the Church for scholarly research," Sperry explained. "I hope to develop young scholars, especially those with a flair for languages." He hoped to make it possible to pursue advanced degrees in the atmosphere of their own religion and not have to travel great distances to do so.[31]

In the fall of 1953 the responsibilities of leadership separated. The major administrative responsibility passed to B. West Belnap, who became director of the Undergraduate Division of Religion. Sperry was appointed to the new office of director of Graduate Studies in Religion.

---

29. *Catalog,* 1958–59, 365.

30. College of Religious Instruction graduate faculty meeting minutes, January 3, 1963.

31. *88th Annual Commencement Convocation,* 24.

1959-70

On January 14, 1959, the Board of Trustees approved changing the Division of Religion to the College of Religious Instruction, headed by a dean. When the division was created in 1940, there were only five people on the religion faculty, and most classes were taught by individuals from other disciplines. With the dramatic expansion of this faculty, however, the religion teachers were able to carry the major load themselves. The expanding graduate offering also argued for college status. Nevertheless, cautioned President McKay, "we must always remember at BYU that religion is to be taught in any and all subjects and not confined to the College of Religion."[1]

---

1.   Ernest L. Wilkinson, memorandum of conference with the First Presidency, January 15, 1959.

David H. Yarn Jr., dean of Religious Instruction, 1959–62. Yarn emphasized revising the course offerings to ensure that, upon graduating, students had been instructed in all areas of the gospel rather than in only one narrow field (see page 32). Courtesy of University Archives, L. Tom Perry Special Collections, Harold B. Lee Library, BYU.

The first dean of the new college was David H. Yarn Jr., a native of Atlanta, Georgia. He earned his doctorate in education in the area of philosophy of religion at Columbia. In addition to years of administrative experience within the Division of Religion, he had served in a stake presidency as well as on both the Sunday School and Young Men's Mutual Improvement Association general boards.

Dean Yarn recalled, "I felt it was good that the division had become a college. We had graduate classes, and certainly that was an important reason for the change. However, there was something more significant. Previous to the change, I felt that the division was regarded as less important than the colleges. The appointment of a dean, I believe, established us on an equal footing with the rest of the university."[2]

The newly formed college immediately took steps to improve its internal organization. In the Division of Religion there had been four departments on the undergraduate level, each with a chairman. At the

2. David H. Yarn, interview by Richard Neitzel Holzapfel, April 22, 2008.

same time, a single director of Graduate Studies in Religion supervised four "areas" that were similar to, but not exactly the same as, the undergraduate departments. In the interest of efficiency, the new organization combined the former undergraduate departments and graduate areas into five subject-area departments, each with a chairman.

College of Religious Instruction
1959

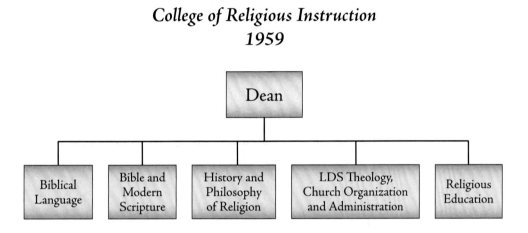

Curriculum Reorganization

BYU's planned shift from the quarter system to semesters in 1960 provided occasion for a thorough review of the religion curriculum. This was the subject of extensive and intensive discussions in college faculty meetings during May, June, and July of 1959. During those deliberations, Dean Yarn reminded the faculty that "one of the purposes of revising the curriculum was to make sure that the courses offered . . . would be of fundamental value to the student." He pointed out that because students take only a limited number of courses in religion, they should be encouraged to study the fundamentals of the gospel rather than narrow their studies to classes in just one field.[3]

A helpful change in numbering courses was made following a suggestion by Daniel H. Ludlow. In the past, confusion had arisen when students registered for "Religion 301," for example, which could have

College of Religious Instruction faculty, spring 1959. (Left to right) **Front row:** *David H. Yarn, Hugh W. Nibley, Rodney Turner, A. Burt Horsley, Daniel H. Ludlow, Ivan J. Barrett, Ellis T. Rasmussen.* **Middle row:** *Truman G. Madsen, B. West Belnap, Roy W. Doxey, Anthony I. Bentley, Lewis Max Rogers, G. Byron Done, James R. Clark.* **Back row:** *Hyrum Andrus, Keith Meservy, Howard H. Barron, J. Grant Stevenson, Chauncey C. Riddle, Sidney B. Sperry, Eldin Ricks.* **Not pictured:** *Reid Bankhead, J. Orval Ellsworth, H. Alvah Fitzgerald, Gustive O. Larson, Glenn L. Pearson, Russell R. Rich. Courtesy of Religious Education.*

---

3. College faculty meeting minutes, May 28, 1959.

been either Scripture 301 (Old Testament) or Church History 301 (LDS history). Ludlow recommended that all such duplicated course numbers be eliminated. Henceforth, the first digit in the course numbers represented the level of the course, first-year through graduate. The second digit indicated the subject areas as follows: 0, Old Testament; 1, New Testament; 2, modern scriptures; 3, theology and organization; 4, LDS history; 5, Christian history and world religion; 6, family history; 7, religious education; 8, philosophy; and 9, special courses, seminars, thesis, dissertation, and so forth. The final digit would identify specific courses.[4]

Over the years an increasing number of courses taught in such areas as archaeology, history, literature, family living, and music were given "cross-reference credit" and could therefore satisfy the religion requirement, simply because they might be related to some aspect of Church activity.[5] However, because the cross-reference credit program was difficult to administer and because the specific objective of the religion requirement was to "give the student a fundamental education of the Gospel of Jesus Christ," university officials decided in 1960 that all such cross-referencing would be discontinued and that only courses taught in the College of Religious Instruction could fill the religion requirement.[6] This decision channeled more students into these regular religion courses.

---

4.   College faculty meeting minutes, April 2, 1959.

5.   Department chair meeting minutes, December 12, 1958.

6.   "Report of Committee on Requirements of Religion and their Relationship to the General Education Requirements," May 1960, 2; Wilkinson to BYU faculty, July 11, 1960.

The Basic Course

The same committee that gave consideration to cross-reference credit also recommended in May 1960 that a new basic course be created "in Doctrines and Principles of the Gospel and Practical LDS Living."[7] While the College of Religious Instruction was taking steps to implement this decision, it was also considering another alternative—that the Book of Mormon be the basic course. The relative merits of each proposal were discussed vigorously and at great length in religion faculty meetings through the remainder of that year.

Those who favored the basic course in theology pointed out that it would provide the complete coverage of gospel principles that students needed. This course should draw from all the scriptures rather than focusing only on one and would provide a desirable broad background for subsequent study of more specific areas, such as the Book of Mormon. On the other hand, those favoring the Book of Mormon course emphasized that this book had been given as the prime instrument for converting people to Christ in this day. Focusing on this impressive book of scripture, these faculty members insisted, would give more weight to moral and ethical principles. Yet advocates of the theology course pointed out that the Book of Mormon does not treat all gospel doctrines; they also feared it could be taught more as a history of the Nephites than as America's witness for Christ.

On March 15, 1961, Elders Harold B. Lee and Marion G. Romney of the Quorum of the Twelve strongly recommended "that the basic

---

7. General Education Committee Report, May 1960, 2.

course required for all freshman at the Brigham Young University and in every other Church School be the 'Book of Mormon.' Since, as the Prophet Joseph Smith said, The Book of Mormon, 'is the keystone of our religion,' we think it should be taught to every student."[8] By May, word of this decision had been relayed to the College of Religious Instruction; preparations then moved forward rapidly to provide enough teachers for the anticipated eighty to ninety Book of Mormon classes that would need to be offered that fall.[9]

B. West Belnap, dean of Religious Instruction, 1962–66. Belnap affirmed that commitment to the gospel is vital. He taught that with respect to qualifications for teachers of religion, a testimony of the restored gospel is indispensable and exceeds scholastic achievement in importance. Courtesy of University Archives, L. Tom Perry Special Collections, Harold B. Lee Library, BYU.

Growth and Direction

In 1962, because of illness, Dean Yarn was given an honorable release from his demanding responsibilities as dean. His successor, B. West Belnap, had served as president of a BYU stake and became executive secretary to one of the Churchwide correlation committees. His commitment to the gospel was reflected in his "Basic Fundamentals for Teachers of Religion." In this document, he

8. Harold B. Lee and Marion G. Romney to the Church Board of Education and BYU Board of Trustees, March 15, 1961.

9. Department chair meeting minutes, May 12, 1961.

College of Religious Instruction
1963

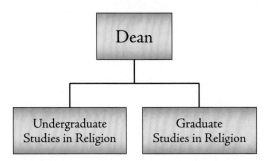

insisted that every teacher have "a testimony of the Gospel as revealed by the power of the Holy Ghost." Teachers should have and be able to communicate an abiding faith in the actuality and literalness of gospel truths including the Fall of Adam, the Atonement and Resurrection of Jesus Christ, Joseph Smith's First Vision and the latter-day Restoration of the gospel, the Book of Mormon's witness for Christ, and the authority of living prophets. He believed that a testimony of these truths is essential, regardless of what scholarship or intellectual attainment we may achieve.[10]

During the four years Belnap was dean, the full-time faculty of the College of Religious Instruction increased from thirty-one to forty-one. This represented an annual growth rate of about double that of previous years. Dean Belnap therefore took steps to simplify the administrative structure.

Dean Belnap underwent brain surgery in May and again in July of 1966 for the removal of a tumor, which proved to be malignant. It was

---

10. Religious Instruction faculty workshop minutes, September 17, 1963.

Daniel H. Ludlow, dean of Religious Instruction, 1967–70. Ludlow's background and experience in education prepared him to make many contributions. He wrote the first syllabus for Book of Mormon (coordinating the efforts of different teachers who taught the same class), explored the use of new media in the classroom, and conducted the first university faculty trips to the Holy Land. Courtesy of University Archives, L. Tom Perry Special Collections, Harold B. Lee Library, BYU.

apparent that his condition would not permit him to carry on his administrative responsibilities, so Roy W. Doxey was named acting dean in August. Dean Belnap died January 13, 1967. His funeral was a fittingly spiritual occasion, with Elder Harold B. Lee of the Quorum of the Twelve as one of the speakers. Members of the College of Religious Instruction faculty were invited to be honorary pallbearers.

Teaching Resources Enhanced

Daniel H. Ludlow became the next dean of Religious Instruction. In addition to being an effective administrator, he was a great teacher and teaching was his first love. He earned his master's degree at the University of Indiana and his doctorate of education at Columbia, both in the field of curriculum materials and teaching. He was one of the original high councilors of the first BYU stake and later served in the stake presidency. In 1960 he was one of four educators whom the General Authorities called to make a comprehensive study of the Church's curriculum and activities; for the next quarter of a century he played a key leadership role in the Church correlation program.

The popularity of basic religion classes required that many sections of each be offered. Providing syllabus materials for these classes was one of the projects which moved forward under Dean Ludlow's leadership. The College of Religious Instruction sponsored these efforts by giving faculty members released time to prepare the various syllabi. The first of these in Book of Mormon had been prepared in 1965 by Dean Ludlow himself, and others followed for the Gospel Principles, Old Testament, New Testament, and Living Prophets courses. Likewise, the college gave released time to Ivan J. Barrett and Russell R. Rich to write their Church history texts.

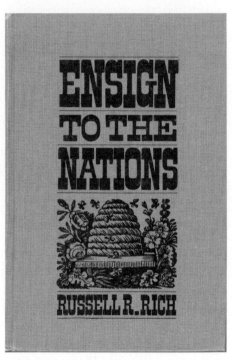

Russell R. Rich's text commissioned by Religious Instruction, Ensign to the Nations *(Provo, UT: Brigham Young University Press, 1972).*

Instructional television was another teaching tool developed under Dean Ludlow's leadership. In the fall of 1965, Book of Mormon became the second BYU course to be taught by television (the basic U.S. history survey course having been offered by TV the year before). Students in three experimental sections viewed two television lectures per week and met one additional hour for discussion with a live teacher. In 1968 the format was changed to include one TV presentation and one live session per week, bringing this course in line with the number of hours spent in other two-credit classes. During that year twenty-eight Church history TV lectures were also developed under the direction of LaMar C. Berrett. Both teachers and students, however, regarded impersonality of the television medium as a particularly serious handicap in teaching religion, where sharing faith and testimony must accompany factual information. Since that time television has been used only in brief segments to enrich regular classes.

Dean Ludlow proposed another important resource for religion teachers. Traditionally faculty members could elect a sabbatical leave of either one year at half salary or one semester at full pay for additional study, often at some other university. However, this released time for additional study was not generally a meaningful option, especially for those teaching uniquely Latter-day Saint subjects. Dean Ludlow, who had experienced the stimulation of travel in the Holy Land, organized a new kind of sabbatical leave consisting of a two-month study tour in the Bible lands with all expenses paid. In the summer of 1968, under the personal leadership of Dean Ludlow, faculty members visited points of interest in Italy, Greece, Turkey, Egypt, Jordan, and Lebanon and spent three weeks in Israel. Similar programs were conducted in subsequent years, and in 1974 Paul R. Cheesman conducted a six-week tour to the lands of the Book of Mormon in Latin America. These programs were forerunners to a wide array of travel-study experiences sponsored for faculty members in later years.

Administration and Curriculum Streamlined

In 1963 the college had been divided into only two departments—Graduate and Undergraduate Studies in Religion—to facilitate scheduling of classes. In 1969, however, a faculty committee recommended the reestablishment of subject-matter departments to maximize opportunities for association and exchange among faculty members sharing a common interest in course content and methodology. Hence the departments of Ancient Scripture, Church History and Doctrine, and Philosophy came into being.[11] Four "area coordinators" were named to give further emphasis to inservice training and mutual strengthening of the faculty in their respective fields.

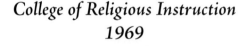

College of Religious Instruction
1969

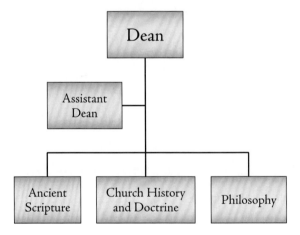

---

11. "Departmental Reorganization and Curriculum Revision of the College of Religious Instruction," committee report, April 24, 1969, 1.

Roy W. Doxey was appointed to the new position of assistant dean with responsibility for such internal matters as classroom teaching and scheduling, while the dean retained responsibility for matters which must be taken to the university administration such as rank, salaries, and leaves. This move now made it possible for the dean to teach classes on a limited basis.

A further streamlining of the curriculum in 1970 followed the principles Dean Yarn had enunciated a decade earlier. While retaining "sufficient latitude in the curriculum to allow for the diversity of background and interest among students," these changes eliminated "duplicate and overlapping courses" that had enabled a student "to concentrate his religious studies in one area at the expense of the remainder of our rich scriptural, historical and doctrinal heritage."[12] The reduction of total undergraduate courses by about one-fourth not only brought greater efficiency but also channeled enrollment into the more basic areas of gospel study.

In 1972 the religion requirement for graduation was clarified. As early as 1913 the faculty had passed a resolution that all students be required to take a class in theology.[13] Then, when the Division of Religion was organized in 1940, the Board of Trustees increased the requirement to two hours of religion for each quarter at BYU.[14] This meant that students should "study religion contemporaneously with . . . other

12. "Departmental Reorganization and Curriculum Revision of the College of Religious Instruction," 2.
13. Faculty minutes, 1913–19, 14.
14. Executive Committee meeting minutes, January 5, 1940.

academic disciplines" rather than "accumulating excessive religion credit in one semester in order to be excused from religion another semester."[15]

At this time the Board of Trustees also modified and clarified the basic religion requirement. In 1972 the board reaffirmed the 1940 requirement of two credit hours for each semester at BYU but reduced the total graduation requirement from sixteen to fourteen semester hours. The granting of credit for attendance at devotionals (which had been allowed on a limited basis since 1960) was discontinued. To avoid "stockpiling" of religion credit, the board specified that only three hours per semester could be counted toward graduation. Finally, to meet the needs especially of seniors and graduate students, varied special one-hour courses or seminars were inaugurated.[16]

---

15. Department chair meeting minutes, February 14, 1961.
16. "Revised Religion Requirement of BYU," May 3, 1972, 1.

The Hub of the University

1970–79

In 1971, when Brother Ludlow was appointed director of instructional materials for the Church, Roy W. Doxey, who had served as assistant or acting dean twice for a total of three years, became dean. Dean Doxey received BA and MA degrees in economics from George Washington University. He presided over the Eastern States Mission, served on the YMMIA general board, and was president of the Provo Stake. In 1972 he became a regional representative of the Twelve. He authored six books, as well as the Relief Society lessons for sixteen years, mostly dealing with the Doctrine and Covenants. Thus, Dean Doxey had especially close contact with the General Authorities for nearly a third of a century.

A New Status for Religious Education

The appropriateness of giving graduate degrees in religion had been a topic of discussion for several years. Those favoring these degrees pointed out the need for seminary and institute teachers to have specialized preparation in the subjects they teach; furthermore, the research done by these graduate students had made a valuable contribution to scholarship and understanding of Latter-day Saint history and theology. Opponents were concerned that professional preparation might eclipse spiritual qualification for teaching religion. A practical problem was that if a person were released from the seminaries and institutes system, a religion degree from BYU would not be very marketable elsewhere. Furthermore, most institute teachers felt their graduate degrees would have more respectability "across the street" if they were not in religion.

On May 3, 1972, the Board of Trustees decided that the College of Religious Instruction would no longer offer doctoral degrees.[1] "This decision could not help producing, in the minds and feelings of many faculty members, several serious questions," noted Elder Packer later. "The way the decision was accepted by the faculty of the college is indeed a remarkable thing in the history of education and in the history of the Church."[2] Minors were to be developed on the master's and doctoral levels, and graduate courses for the benefit of seminary or institute personnel continued to be offered on the BYU campus or at other locations as needed.[3]

1. "Revised Religion Requirement of BYU," 2.
2. Packer, "Seek Learning," 31.
3. Dallin H. Oaks to Roy W. Doxey, June 21, 1972.

Early in 1973, university leaders suggested that Religious Instruction drop the designation "college." There never had been undergraduate majors in religion, and now graduate degrees in this area were being phased out. Furthermore, Religious Instruction should be a unit providing service for the entire university rather than just another academic college. Some religion teachers feared, however, that the loss of college status would substantially lessen the prestige and hence, the importance of Religious Instruction in the eyes of the faculty, students, and Church membership in general.

If Religious Instruction was not to be a college, what was it to be? This question was considered thoughtfully by university and college administrators. "Department" status was rejected because religious instruction includes more areas and provides a much broader service than that usually identified with other univer-

Roy W. Doxey, dean of Religious Instruction, 1971–74. Under Doxey's direction, faculty members of Religious Instruction and of the physical and biological sciences met together to inform and enrich each other's understanding of their respective fields in areas of common interest, such as the Creation account. Courtesy of University Archives, L. Tom Perry Special Collections, Harold B. Lee Library, BYU.

sity departments. "Division of Religion" was declined because Religious Instruction was not comparable with other university divisions and because the name might be said, tongue in cheek, to reflect a disunity that does not exist. Religious Instruction was not an "institute," as that designation on other university campuses normally refers to temporary programs. Furthermore, Church members think of institutes of religion as being adjacent to and completely detached from universities. The solution was to suit the name to the function and refer to this unit simply as "Religious Instruction." Roy W. Doxey would retain the title "dean" and continue to be a member of the deans' council. At about this time, Evelyn Scheiss filled the new position of administrative assistant to the dean. As part of Religious Instruction's change in status, the Department of Philosophy was transferred to the College of General Studies. This left the two departments which would characterize the organization for at least a quarter of a century.

BYU president Dallin H. Oaks declared: "This move emphasizes the prominence of religious education of BYU by affirming its centrality to the University and erasing the restrictive college boundary." Religion classes would continue to be taught primarily by the full-time faculty of Religious Instruction, but, to an increasing extent, qualified faculty members from other colleges across campus would also be called on to instruct these classes. "The teaching of religion is a university-wide concern which will be fostered by a university-wide jurisdiction,"

Dallin H. Oaks, president of Brigham Young University, 1971–80. During his tenure, Religious Instruction ceased to be its own college, reflecting its mission to enhance all areas of education in the university. An increased percentage of religion classes were taught by faculty members from other colleges. © Intellectual Reserve, Inc.

President Oaks declared. It would make it easier to involve faculty from throughout the university in the teaching of religion. President Oaks pointed out, "Scholarship in religious subjects is widespread throughout the faculty since the LDS Church is administered by a lay priesthood, and lifelong study and teaching of scriptures and doctrines is encouraged and practiced. Consequently, . . . many professors are preeminently qualified to teach religious subjects as well as their particular academic disciplines." Therefore, President Oaks explained, whenever faculty members are employed by BYU, in whatever department, they should also be considered as potential teachers of religion. In 1973 about 10 percent of all religion classes were taught by faculty from other colleges; President Oaks anticipated that this might be increased to about 20 percent in the foreseeable future. President Oaks affirmed, however, "We shall, of course, continue to depend on full-time faculty in Religious Instruction for the leadership and scholarship necessary to improve further our effectiveness in the teaching of religion."[4] Elder Packer concurred, insisting that the board never even considered the possibility of doing away with the full-time religion faculty. "Your work has now moved from *a* college to *the* University," he emphasized.[5]

Typical of these efforts to break down barriers was a series of science and religion seminars. These had been initiated in 1971 under the direction of Dean Doxey and were conducted by Ellis Rasmussen, the assistant dean. A selected group of faculty members from Religious Instruction, as well as from the physical and biological sciences, met regularly to discuss

4. *Daily Universe*, June 12, 1973, 1.
5. Packer, "Seek Learning," 32; emphasis added.

issues of common interest. "When these groups get together, they not only come to understand each other better," Rasmussen believed, "but they also enrich one another. There are discoveries in the physical and biological sciences which we in Religion should understand, and there are technicalities of doctrine and scriptural history which they probably would not know." For example, the group was fascinated to learn the connotations of Hebrew words used in the Genesis account of the Creation, as explained by Dr. Rasmussen.[6]

"Senior Seminars in Religion" were another means by which colleges across campus participated in religious instruction. These one-credit classes were taught by experts in the sciences, humanities, or business, who explained how they correlated the gospel with their respective disciplines. First offered during the 1973–74 academic year, these Religion 490 seminars were under the supervision of the Department of Church History and Doctrine. In later years some colleges expanded their offering to two credits.

Religion at the Hub of the University

Upon Dean Doxey's retirement, Jeffrey R. Holland was appointed dean of Religious Instruction on January 11, 1974. Though only thirty-three at the time of his appointment, Dean Holland had earned a PhD in American studies at Yale University, had served as a bishop and as a member of a stake presidency, and had directed the institute adjacent to the University of Washington. At the time of his call, he was director of the Melchizedek Priesthood MIA Churchwide. Elder Packer testified

6.   Ellis T. Rasmussen, interview by Richard O. Cowan, June 22, 1981.

that this appointment had been made by the board through inspiration; "mostly it was done in the way a bishop is chosen, or a stake president, or a General Authority."[7]

At the outset of his service, Dean Holland affirmed his determination to do all possible to advance the dignity, stature, and importance of teaching religion at BYU. He believed that the end of college status had "opened the gates" for religion to become "an influence everywhere on the campus."[8] He visited deans, department leaders, and key scholars across campus. In a friendly and informal manner, he sought to convince them that religion was not the function of just one college but rather of the whole university. It was at the heart of BYU's unique contribution, and all other faculties should feel that they had a responsibility in it. Dean Holland declared: "To me it is a great new era to see the possibility of religious discussion permeating the University."[9]

Jeffrey R. Holland, dean of Religious Education, 1974–76. Dean Holland assured that Religious Education's new status would increase, not decrease, its influence. Religion faculty members conducted seminars and symposia, both in-house and campuswide, to share teaching ideas and current research, aiding the numerous teachers from other colleges who began teaching religion classes. © Intellectual Reserve, Inc.

7. Packer, "Seek Learning," 32.
8. Jeffrey R. Holland, interview by Richard O. Cowan, May 7, 1976.
9. *Daily Universe*, June 21, 1974.

As part of this broadened emphasis, the "transfer faculty" program was promoted. By 1976 the share of classes taught by members of other departments increased from 9 to 22 percent. The number of cross-campus faculty members grew from about thirty-five to eighty-five. The plan was to rotate these teachers so more could have the opportunity.

Religious Instruction faculty, October 1978. **Front Row:** *Douglas Boden, Larry C. Porter, Ellis T. Rasmussen, Robert J. Matthews, Rodney Turner, Larry E. Dahl, Reed A. Benson, A. Burt Horsley, James R. Harris, Hal Taylor, Lyndon W. Cook.* **Row 2:** *A. Gary Anderson, Leon R. Hartshorn, Robert Parsons, Richard O. Cowan, Frank Gonzales, Victor L. Ludlow, Blaine M. Yorgason, Brenton G. Yorgason, Grant Shields, Roger Gull.* **Row 3:** *Leaun G. Otten, Monte S. Nyman, James R. Moss, James R. Christianson, Joseph F. McConkie, Melvin J. Petersen, Richard L. Anderson, David J. Whittaker, Keith W. Perkins.* **Row 4:** *Leonard Carter, Keith H. Meservy, Wilson K. Andersen, Paul Felt, Milton V. Backman Jr., Howard H. Barron, Donald Q. Cannon, Paul Edwards Damron, C. Max Caldwell, J. Spencer Palmer.* **Row 5:** *J. Grant Stevenson, Paul R. Cheesman, John P. Fugal, John Child, H. Donl Peterson, LaMar E. Garrard, Clark V. Johnson, Terry R. Baker. Courtesy of Religious Education.*

Responsibility for administering this growing program was delegated to assistant dean Ellis T. Rasmussen. He supervised the work of all part-time teachers, including the transfer faculty, visiting seminary and institute teachers, graduate students, and selected individuals from off campus. He also coordinated schedules and budgets with other departments and with the Church Educational System (CES).

One of the visiting CES teachers, Juan Henderson, worked on his graduate degree while teaching part-time.

Area coordinators also assumed a more important role. They conducted regular seminars for teachers of each subject to share background information, teaching ideas, or results from current research. These efforts were especially valuable in Book of Mormon and gospel principles classes, where there were more transfer teachers.

Former director Darin Palmer evaluated candidates for Church Educational System slots assisted by Aaronita Openshaw. Courtesy of Richard B. Crookston.

Dean Holland assured the full-time faculty that there was no danger of their services or existence being phased out, and he sought to help them feel more comfortable in religion's new campuswide role. "At the Church's university, Religion is at the hub of the wheel," he declared. He emphasized that there should be no tension between teachers of religion and scholars in other fields.[10]

Some faculty members felt that they were so busy teaching classes or working on their own projects that they did not have enough time for interaction with one another. To remedy this, a Friday noon "brown bag seminar" was launched during the 1974–75 school year. Faculty members took turns leading gospel discussions, reporting research, or seeking feedback on articles then in preparation. These sessions, generally "in-house," were intended to give the faculty a greater opportunity simply to "hear one another."[11]

During these years Religious Instruction sought to reach out more effectively to the broader campus community and beyond. The family of Sidney B. Sperry had established a research fund in his honor to promote original research of general interest.[12] In 1973 the annual Sperry Lecture Series was inaugurated. In 1975 it featured not only a member of the Religious Instruction faculty but also a professor from another department on campus as well as a scholar from CES, beyond BYU. This was the beginning of a greater "outreach to the entire religious education community."[13] Furthermore, for the first time, the proceedings of the Sperry Lecture Series were published.

In November 1975, the Department of Ancient Scripture sponsored the first annual Fall Symposium. The Saturday program focused on the Pearl of Great Price. Presenters included five from the religion faculty as

10. Holland interview.
11. Holland interview.
12. *Sperry Lecture Series* (Provo, UT: Brigham Young University Press, 1975), iii.
13. Holland interview.

well as the editor of the *Ensign* and an institute member. About a thousand people attended, and the resulting publication enhanced "the image of good orthodox scholarship at BYU."[14]

In April 1976, Dean Holland was named commissioner of education for the Church.[15] His successor was Ellis T. Rasmussen, a longtime faculty member who had been serving as assistant dean for five years. Under Dean Rasmussen's leadership, the emphasis on Religious Instruction's broadened role continued.

Dean Rasmussen continued a close working relationship with CES. In previous decades, separate and often similar manuals were prepared for the institutes and for BYU. Dean Holland and CES administrator Joe J. Christensen believed that working together would benefit both groups and would be far more economical. BYU faculty members with relevant areas of expertise were given reduced teaching loads so they could participate on writing committees. Between 1977 and 1981, new course manuals

Ellis T. Rasmussen, dean of Religious Education, 1976–81. Rasmussen coordinated efforts between BYU and the Church Educational System, reducing duplication by producing religion manuals that would be used by both organizations. BYU symposia were also expanded to serve as in-service trainings for CES personnel. Courtesy of University Archives, L. Tom Perry Special Collections, Harold B. Lee Library, BYU.

---

14. Holland interview.
15. *Church News*, April 24, 1976, 3.

appeared for LDS Marriage and Family, Sharing the Gospel, New Testament, Book of Mormon, Old Testament, Living Prophets, and Presidents of the Church. A Doctrine and Covenants manual was also nearing publication.[16]

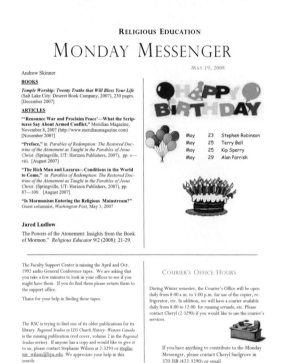

In 1978 the Sperry Lecture was expanded into an all-day symposium. The number of presenters increased from two or three to fourteen. For the first time, a General Authority, Elder Mark E. Petersen of the Quorum of the Twelve, gave the keynote address. Beginning that year the symposium was sponsored jointly by Religious Instruction and by CES. It was intended not only to benefit the university and local communities but also to be a mid-year "in-service enrichment experience for full-time teachers of religion."[17]

Efforts to enhance communication within Religious Instruction continued. Beginning in the fall of 1980, the weekly *Monday Messenger* shared announcements, biographical sketches, and brief thoughts.

---

16. Ellis T. Rasmussen, interview with Richard O. Cowan, June 22, 1981.
17. Sidney B. Sperry Symposium, January 28, 1978, iii.

Research Institutes Sponsored

The Sperry and Fall Lecture Series were only part of Religious Instruction's efforts to promote research. Beginning in 1961, Religious Instruction sponsored the research-oriented Institute of Mormon Studies to examine Mormonism's "unique contributions" in various fields. Daniel H. Ludlow, then chairman of the Department of Bible and Modern Scriptures, was named first director.[18] Dr. Truman G. Madsen, who succeeded him in 1966, described it as "an interuniversity institute" that sponsored and published research "in all fields that relate to Mormon culture, its history, thought, and institutions."[19]

The institute researched and microfilmed source material for the history of the Church in New York, Ohio, and Missouri. It sponsored research by more than fifty separate individuals, in several cases leading to significant publications. Early examples included Milton V. Backman's work on the historical setting for the First Vision and Richard L. Anderson's treatise of Joseph Smith's New England heritage. From 1969 to 1972, the institute cooperated in the preparation of special annual issues of *BYU Studies*, focusing on the Church in New York and Ohio.

In 1965 a separate Institute of Book of Mormon Projects (later renamed the Book of Mormon Institute) was established to promote and coordinate research related to this book of scripture. Daniel H. Ludlow, who had prepared extensive curriculum materials related to the Book of Mormon, also became the first director of this unit.[20] In 1968

---

18. *Daily Universe*, May 15, 1961, 1.
19. Statement prepared by Truman G. Madsen, 1972.
20. Department chair meeting minutes, June 30, 1965.

Hugh Nibley, director of the Institute for Ancient Studies, 1973–77. Well known for his intellect and enthusiasm, Nibley's many publications led to his becoming a recognized name among Latter-day Saints even outside of academia. Photo by Mark Philbrick/BYU.

he was succeeded by Paul R. Cheesman, who had conducted numerous expeditions to important archaeological sites in North and South America. Institute projects included examining ancient metal plates, collecting data on the cultural background of ancient America, and translating the Book of Mormon into Hebrew as well as some of the leading Indian languages of Central and South America.[21] In 1972 Dr. Cheesman produced and narrated a half-hour color motion picture, *Ancient America Speaks*.

Religious Instruction was a cosponsor of the Institute for Ancient Studies, organized in 1973. Hugh Nibley, of the Department of Ancient Scripture, was named director, with R. Douglas Phillips, of the Department of Classical Languages, as associate director. The new institute developed and disseminated "information about ancient manuscripts of religious significance." Dr. Nibley explained that "the scholarly world is being flooded with newly discovered manuscripts, many of which have a direct bearing

---

21. College faculty meeting minutes, January 16, 1968; *Daily Universe*, March 10, 1970.

on the Church. It is important that LDS scholars have and know these manuscripts."[22] The institute was housed in the Harold B. Lee Library.

Religious Studies Center Inaugurated

Organized in 1975, the Religious Studies Center (RSC) built on the foundations laid by these earlier institutes. It absorbed the work being done by the Book of Mormon Institute and the Institute of Mormon Studies, which were discontinued. BYU president Dallin H. Oaks explained that the new center would "be a supporting and coordinating agency for all religion-oriented research" campuswide. The RSC would attract donations of funds which could be channeled into various research projects. It would also facilitate publication of the results from these research efforts.

Dean Holland became the director of the RSC. The center was divided into four subject areas, each headed by an assistant director: Church history, LaMar C. Berrett; scripture, Paul R. Cheesman (who had been serving as director of the Book of Mormon Institute); world religions, Spencer J. Palmer; and Judeo-Christian religions, Truman G. Madsen. This organization would be modified in the future from time to time. Members of the center's advisory board included Daniel H. Ludlow, original director of the former institutes; Joe J. Christensen, of CES; Leonard J. Arrington, Church historian; and Charles D. Tate Jr., editor of *BYU Studies*.[23]

---

22. *Church News*, June 2, 1973, 12.
23. *Daily Universe*, February 27, 1976.

The RSC sponsored annual symposia. The first, in April 1977, centered on "Deity, Ways of Worship, and Death." Presenters included BYU religion professors as well as experts from as far away as Japan and Sri Lanka.[24]

Many significant publications have been sponsored by the RSC. The first volume the RSC published was *Nibley on the Timely and the Timeless*. Other volumes have incorporated papers from various RSC-sponsored symposia, includ-

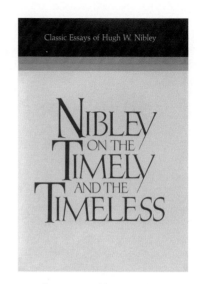

Hugh W. Nibley, Nibley on the Timely and the Timeless *(Provo, UT: Religious Studies Center, BYU, 1978)*

ing nine volumes generated by the annual Book of Mormon symposium. One of the most significant publications of the RSC to date may well be the contemporary accounts of the Nauvoo discourses of the Prophet Joseph Smith, *The Words of Joseph Smith*, edited by Andrew F. Ehat and Lyndon W. Cook. Both Ehat and Cook had received research grants from the RSC and had taught part-time for Religious Education. Truman G. Madsen, who held the Evans chair at the time, opined that for all Latter-day Saints, whether teachers, parents, or scholars, "This book is not only useful, it is indispensable."[25]

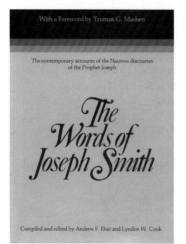

Andrew F. Ehat and Lyndon W. Cook, eds., The Words of Joseph Smith *(Provo, UT: Religious Studies Center, Brigham Young University, 1980), xiv.*

24. *Daily Universe*, April 13, 1977.

25. Andrew F. Ehat and Lyndon W. Cook, eds., *The Words of Joseph Smith* (Provo, UT: Religious Studies Center, Brigham Young University, 1980), xiv.

Evans Chair Established

The establishment of the Richard L. Evans Chair of Christian Understanding and the appointment of Truman G. Madsen to be the first occupant of the chair was announced in November 1972. Elder Evans had been a member of the Quorum of the Twelve Apostles and was probably best known as the voice for *Music and the Spoken Word* in conjunction with the weekly Tabernacle Choir broadcasts.

Courtesy of Richard B. Crookston.

The idea for such a chair had been proposed by Lowell W. Berry, a member of another faith who had been closely associated with Elder

In his former role as an Evans professor, Robert L. Millet (right) discussed Latter-day Saint views with many representatives of other faiths. Those friendships continue today.

Evans in Rotary affairs and who had been profoundly impressed with his commitment to Christianity. Mr. Berry was the first of fifty individuals who contributed to the six hundred thousand dollars necessary to endow such a professional chair. The chair would be occupied by "a distinguished scholar of Brigham Young University" who would promote Christ-centered "understanding among people of differing religious faiths."

This appointment enabled Dr. Madsen, a professor of philosophy, to function as a "commuting professor" by underwriting travel to centers of religious learning, academic conferences, and civic or social gatherings, where he could present Latter-day Saint philosophy and history.[26]

Susan Easton Black began teaching religion classes in the fall of 1976, eventually accepting a full-time appointment in 1981, making her the first full-time female faculty member in Religious Education. Since her appointment she has won numerous accolades, including the Karl G. Maeser Distinguished Faculty Lecturer, the university's most prestigious award, in August 2000. Photo by Mark Philbrick/BYU.

26. *Church News*, November 4, 1972, 5.

Reaching beyond the Classroom

1980–2000

The appointment of Robert J. Matthews as dean of Religious Instruction was announced in May 1981. Having served six years as chairman of the Department of Ancient Scripture, he was well acquainted with Religious Instruction's objectives and functions, and he was virtually the unanimous choice of the faculty. He was a popular speaker and qualified writer, having served as editor for the Church Educational System. Because of his service on the committee producing new editions of the standard works, he was well acquainted with the General Authorities and their views. At a special faculty meeting, he set the tone for his leadership by counseling the faculty: "All should work

Robert J. Matthews, dean of Religious Education, 1981–90. Matthews encouraged faculty members to write and publish more in order to refine and strengthen the ideas they taught. He cautioned that this practice should not preclude relying on modern revelation or serving the needs of students. Photo by Mark Philbrick/BYU.

with an eye single to the glory of God. If we do this, we will succeed. If we work with an eye single to our glory alone, we will not succeed."[1]

Name Changed to Religious Education

By 1983 the name "Religious Instruction" was changed to "Religious Education" because members of this unit do far more than classroom instructing. Furthermore, the new name would parallel the two other campuswide programs of General Education and Honors Education.

The university began placing greater emphasis on writing as part of its quest for increased academic excellence. Dean Matthews concurred, noting that we can reach only a few hundred in the classroom but many thousands through our writings. Furthermore, he asserted, "it is amazing how much clearer our views become, and how quickly we can discover to ourselves what we don't know about a subject when we try to write. . . . We know from expe-

---

1. Religious Instruction faculty meeting minutes, May 7, 1981, 2.

rience that when we set out to compose a document, we nearly always have to do more study, more research, and refine our thinking."[2]

The Religious Education faculty felt it was their opportunity and responsibility to provide quality research and writing that would benefit the whole Church. However, opportunities to publish articles on the restored gospel in scholarly journals were limited. Religious Education took steps to create more outlets for the scholarly work of its faculty. The annual Sperry Symposium was enlarged, including as many as sixteen faculty presentations. Beginning in 1985 the Religious Studies Center began sponsoring an additional annual symposium during winter semester; these treated varied topics of a more scholarly nature. That same year the RSC launched the annual fall Book of Mormon Symposium, which typically included fourteen faculty presentations. A "Research and Writing Committee" was organized to encourage faculty members to take advantage of these opportunities and to provide peer review and editorial assistance when requested. To help teachers keep focused on the spiritual component of their work, Religious Education compiled and distributed five Foundational Documents setting forth counsel by key Church leaders (see excerpts, appendix A).

Selecting new faculty members for Religious Education posed a unique challenge. They needed to meet the general scholarly expectations applied to those teaching in any other area of the university. At the same time, Dean Matthews insisted, they must possess the inclination and ability to build faith in their students. Not only did the usual scholarly credentials need to be examined, but the candidate's experience or

---

2.   Robert J. Matthews, address to Religious Education faculty, August 25, 1987, 2.

Donald Q. Cannon: acting dean, 1990–91, associate dean, 1986–90, 1991–97.

potential as an effective teacher must also be considered.

Dean Matthews raised a related concern: "How do we meet the challenge of increased research and writing and still retain our patience and interest in student needs and welfare? If we are not careful, students could become an *annoyance* to us. If we feel that happening too frequently, we may want to check our priorities."[3]

As administrative duties became increasingly weighty, Dean Matthews revived the position of associate (formerly assistant) dean. Monte S. Nyman was called to this office in 1982 and assumed responsibility for the transfer faculty program. As even more help became necessary, a second associate dean, Donald Q. Cannon, was appointed in 1986. One of his major responsibilities was supervision of research in general and the RSC in particular.

Beginning in 1983, Religious Education provided help to those from other departments who had been invited to teach religion classes. Monte Nyman organized a six-week seminar on the Book of Mormon. Experienced members of the full-time faculty were invited to treat a given group of chapters, not only discussing their content but also modeling effective

----

3. Robert J. Matthews, address to Religious Education faculty, August 28, 1985, 21.

teaching methods. One enthusiastic seminar participant remarked: "It's terrific! It is one of the most stimulating things I have ever done."[4]

Jeffrey R. Holland, who had become BYU's president in 1980, gratefully acknowledged the seminars' "profound effect" across campus. He praised them as having "a collegial, professional influence on the faculty. . . . It is not easy," he conceded, "to walk into a room of professional peers at the University and say, 'I am now going to teach you.' But you have done it in an absolutely terrific way."[5] A similar seminar was later organized for those teaching the Doctrine and Covenants.

The Department of Church History and Doctrine in 1985 launched a series of in-depth visits to areas important in Latter-day Saint history. Faculty members were invited to research facets of the history in

Religious Education
1986

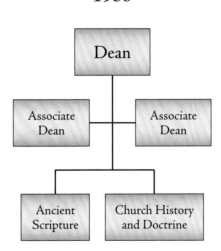

4. *Daily Universe*, June 13, 1990.
5. Meeting with Religious Education faculty, November 10, 1988.

each area. Resulting papers were published in a series of volumes titled *Regional Studies in Latter-day Saint Church History*. The Department of Ancient Scripture organized similar trips to the lands of the Bible and Book of Mormon.

Religious Education faculty, March 10, 1987. (Left to right) **Front row:** *James R. Christianson, Susan Easton Black, Kent P. Jackson, James R. Harris, Robert J. Matthews, Robert L. Millet, Keith W. Perkins, Rodney Turner, Larry E. Dahl, E. Dale LeBaron.* **Row 2:** *Stephen E. Robinson, George A. Horton Jr., LaMar C. Berrett, Donald Q. Cannon, S. Kent Brown, Richard O. Cowan, Keith H. Meservy, Reed A. Benson.* **Row 3:** *S. Michael Wilcox, Wilson K. Andersen, Joseph F. McConkie, Paul Y. Hoskisson, Leon R. Hartshorn, H. Dean Garrett, C. Max Caldwell, Monte S. Nyman.* **Row 4:** *Dennis L. Largey, LaMar E. Garrard, Victor L. Ludlow, H. Donl Peterson, Clark V. Johnson, A. Gary Anderson, Bruce A. Van Orden.* **Row 5:** *Alan K. Parrish, Robert E. Parsons, Larry C. Porter, Richard L. Anderson, Paul H. Peterson, Spencer J. Palmer, Milton V. Backman Jr., J. Grant Stevenson. Courtesy of Religious Education.*

Beginning in the fall of 1985, graduating BYU students were required to have at least one course in the New Testament and another in the Doctrine and Covenants in addition to the basic two-semester Book of Mormon series. Adoption of this "core curriculum" guaranteed that students would be exposed to at least three of the four standard works with

Church history faculty members visiting Pratt's Hill overlooking Edinburgh, Scotland, in 2006. Courtesy of Richard B. Crookston.

emphasis on the scriptures of the Restoration. Inevitably, however, this move led to smaller enrollments in other areas such as Old Testament or Church history.

This shift in emphasis toward the Restoration was also reflected in the RSC in 1989. The former "scripture" area was divided into separate areas for the Bible, Book of Mormon, Doctrine and Covenants, and Pearl of Great Price. At the same time, the Ancient Studies area once again became physically separate from the RSC and was housed in the Harold B. Lee Library.

During these years the far-reaching influence of Religious Education faculty members was felt in new ways. During the fall of 1985, over a million visitors toured the Ramses II exhibit at the Monte L. Bean Museum. The favorable impression C. Wilfred Griggs had made on

Egyptian officials led to BYU's becoming the first U.S. institution invited to host this dazzling collection of ancient artifacts.[6]

BYU Jerusalem Center

From the beginning, the religion faculty has played a key part in Brigham Young University's programs in the Holy Land. The first study tour there was led in 1953 by Sidney B. Sperry, director of the Division of Religion. He was assisted by Eldin Ricks, another member of the religion faculty. In 1966 the First Presidency approved a semester abroad in Jerusalem with the provision that equal attention be given to the Arabs and the Jews, but the Six-Day War the following year delayed implementation.

The Jerusalem Center for Near Eastern Studies. Photo by Mark Philbrick/BYU.

---

6. *Daily Universe,* August 6, 1985.

In January 1968, Daniel H. Ludlow, dean of Religious Instruction, took a group of twenty students to Jerusalem. Dean Ludlow, realizing members of his faculty would not benefit much from a traditional sabbatical leave, proposed an alternative. During the summer of 1968, he led the two-month "Lands of the Scriptures" workshop, including three weeks in Israel. As the approximately two dozen professors held a priesthood meeting on the slopes of the Mount of Olives, they realized they were the largest group of Melchizedek Priesthood bearers in the Holy Land since the time of the Savior.

Under the direction of BYU's Travel Study office, other student semesters abroad followed. One or more members of the religion faculty regularly directed these groups and taught courses in the Old and New Testaments. These groups were typically housed in youth hostels or on kibbutzim, so there was a definite need for a permanent home. The result was the 135,000-square-foot BYU Jerusalem Center for Near Eastern Studies, which opened in 1987. This beautiful facility on eight levels became a recognized landmark on the slope of Mount Scopus and afforded spectacular views of the Old City.

The purpose of the center was twofold: (1) to provide a unique opportunity to study the Bible as well as Near Eastern languages, cultures, and history in their native lands and (2) to establish cultural and service programs to benefit the Holy Land and its peoples.[7]

Upon moving to this new facility, the Jerusalem program expanded to include courses in the ancient and modern Near East, classes in Hebrew and Arabic, and the traditional Bible classes. Instruction was enhanced

---

7. *The Jerusalem Center for Near Eastern Studies* (Provo, UT: Brigham Young University, 2000).

by frequent fieldtrips to key biblical sites. Faculty members who actually taught the classes were assisted by administrators and a support staff. Members of the religion faculty continued to play an important part. In 1989 George Horton became the first of four from this faculty appointed consecutively to direct the Jerusalem Center for a total of nine years.

As tensions in the world increased, the center was closed at the end of the year 2000. As the climate stabilized, however, students once again returned to the center in 2007. Even though the staff was streamlined in comparison to earlier years, the number of religion teachers at the center remained about the same. With so many religion teachers in Jerusalem, the faculty in Provo needed to cover their classes; this they were willing to do because of the great benefit the experience in the Holy Land provided to their colleagues as well as to the students.

The New Joseph Smith Building

In the 1960s, the basic functions of the Joseph Smith Building underwent major changes. When the Harris Fine Arts Center opened in 1964, dramatic productions were no longer staged in the JSB auditorium. With the completion of the Ernest L. Wilkinson Center the following year, the JSB was no longer needed as a social and recreational center for the campus. Both the basement area formerly occupied by the cafeteria and also the large ballroom of the main floor were remodeled to provide additional classrooms and office space. For the first time in many years, almost the entire full-time religion faculty, many of whom had for some time been located in temporary buildings around campus, could be housed under one roof.

These remodelings, however, left the building with some significant problems. Fitting so many offices into these former spacious rooms resulted in confusing passageways. Because most campus growth had occurred toward the north, the thousands of students coming to the JSB for religion classes each hour had to thread their way through this maze of narrow hallways rather than use the commodious entrance on the west. Furthermore, there were no elevators to give students with disabilities access to the offices in the basement or to the two separate and unconnected floors, where all but three of the classrooms were located.

Making way for a new Joseph Smith Building. Photo by Mark Philbrick/BYU.

BYU officials announced on January 31, 1989, the decision to construct a new building. The new structure would have approximately the same area as the old and hence was to be regarded as a replacement rather than as an enlargement.

The assignment of designing the new Joseph Smith Building was given to the architectural firm of John and Dix Markham, sons of Fred L. Markham, the designer of the original structure a half century earlier. Their plans blended features of the old building into a new architectural design. The sixty thousand square feet of floor space included a nine-hundred-seat auditorium, seventeen classrooms,

The Joseph Smith Building. Built from 1989 to 1991, the new building completely replaced the former Joseph Smith Building, which had occupied the same spot of ground. While the former building contained a cafeteria and a ballroom, serving a variety of purposes, the new building served to house the previously dispersed religion faculty, as well as provide areas for gospel-centered displays and quiet reflection for the students. Courtesy of L. Tom Perry Special Collections, Harold B. Lee Library, BYU.

seventy-five offices, as well as conference rooms, a student commons area, and other facilities.[8]

A bronze sculpture facing the quad to the north honored Joseph Smith. Sculpted by artist Franz Johansen, the twenty-five-by-nine-foot panel depicted the Prophet teaching a young family the doctrines of the kingdom out of the scriptures.

President Gordon B. Hinckley dedicated the new Joseph Smith Building on December 10, 1991. BYU president Rex E. Lee affirmed,

---

8. *Daily Universe*, November 30, 1989.

"Joseph Smith's life and work are as central to the Restoration, and to the welfare of humankind, as the learning that will occur in this building is central to the mission of our university."[9] As he dedicated the building, President Gordon B. Hinckley petitioned:

Dedication of the Joseph Smith Building, December 10, 1991. The dignitaries include President Gordon B. Hinckley, Marjorie Pay Hinckley, Larry E. Dahl, Robert L. Millet, Donald Q. Cannon, Janet Lee, and Rex E. Lee. Franz Johansen's relief sculpture portrays Joseph Smith standing among Latter-day Saints as light falls from heaven. A phrase from D&C 88:77–78 accompanies the figures. "The phrase 'teach ye diligently and my grace shall attend you' captures BYU's complete mission, combining the relentless pursuit of intellectual diligence with unwavering faith in the gospel and grace of Jesus Christ. . . . Could it possibly be that if our teaching is diligent enough and if our eyes really are single to God's glory, the grace of the holy atonement would attend us? . . . Franz Johansen lifts my eyes to look for the answers with the powerful lines of grace and light that he carved streaming from heaven in the new relief sculpture at the Joseph Smith Building" (Bruce C. Hafen, "Teach Ye Diligently and My Grace Shall Attend You," August 25, 1993, speeches.byu.edu). Courtesy of L. Tom Perry Special Collections, Harold B. Lee Library, BYU.

---

9.   *Y News,* April 6, 1990, 1.

The Joseph Smith Building became a popular place to study. Courtesy of Richard B. Crookston.

We pray for those who will walk its halls and sit in its classrooms, that their minds may be enlightened, that their understanding may be quickened, that they may learn those things which will bless their lives in the world of which they will become a part, and, in a more particular way, that they will become familiar with that truth which is eternal in its nature and everlasting in its consequences.

Bless the faculty who will teach here that they may be qualified through scholarship to do so effectively, but, more important, that they may teach by the power of the Holy Spirit, that their faith may be strengthened, that truth shall be established, and that thy divine will may be done. . . .

Let thy Holy Spirit abide constantly within these walls and be felt by all who teach and learn. May there be an absence of intellectual arrogance; rather, may there be that humility which comes of recognition that man, with all of his knowledge and understanding, shares only a feeble light when compared with the wisdom of the Almighty.[10]

A statue depicting Joseph Smith at the time of his First Vision was placed in the building's atrium in 1997. This sculpture, titled *The Vision*,

---

10. *Joseph Smith Memorial Building Dedication Remarks*, 1.

Unveiling of "The Vision," by Avard T. Fairbanks. At the dedication of the bronze sculpture on October 17, 1997, Elder Henry B. Eyring said, "One of the marks of great art is not what it portrays but what it suggests. There are other figures not sculpted here which I would like you to imagine with an eye of faith. God the Eternal Father and his Beloved Son Jesus Christ appeared to open this dispensation." Courtesy of Richard O. Cowan.

was a gift from the classes of 1945, 1947, 1955, and 1957. The statue was an original made by well-known sculptor Avard T. Fairbanks, who had hoped that a bronze cast could be placed where it would "solemnly tell the story of the beginning of the restoration of the gospel."[11] At the unveiling ceremony, Elder Henry B. Eyring of the Quorum of the Twelve acknowledged that even "though the building is named for Joseph Smith, and though the statue portrays him, this piece of art represents that moment

---

11. *Joseph Smith Memorial Building Dedication Remarks*, 16–17.

Robert L. Millet, dean of Religious Education, 1991–2000. Millet counseled faculty to avoid the cynicism and arrogance that can so often accompany religious scholarship. He and several BYU faculty visited other religious universities such as Notre Dame to build relations and observe their approach to religious education. Photo by Mark Philbrick/BYU.

when Joseph learned that there is a way for the power of the Atonement of Jesus Christ to be unlocked fully."[12]

Outreach Extended

Robert J. Matthews was one of the senior editors working on the *Encyclopedia of Mormonism*. As pressures from this assignment mounted, he was released as dean in January 1990. Donald Q. Cannon, who had served four years as associate dean, was named acting dean. After a year, Robert L. Millet was named as dean. After receiving his doctorate at Florida State University in biblical studies and nineteenth- and twentieth-century religious thought, he joined the Religious Education faculty in 1983. At the time of his appointment as dean, he was serving as department chair of ancient scripture.

Three members of the Quorum of the Twelve Apostles attended the meeting where Dean Millet was introduced—Elder Neal A. Maxwell, chairman of the executive committee of the board; Elder Dallin H. Oaks, a former president of BYU; and Elder Boyd K. Packer, who had a long-standing background and interest in Church education. Their pres-

12. "Remarks Given at the Unveiling Ceremony of 'The Vision,'" typescript, October 17, 1997.

ence evidenced the importance the Brethren attached to the teaching of religion at BYU. "If the Religious Education faculty were not doing what they are doing," affirmed Elder Oaks, this "would not be the Lord's University." Speaking to the faculty, Elder Packer explained, "We came down to honor you for your work."[13]

Elder Maxwell counseled the new dean to seek new ways to reach out to and bless the broader Church and even the world as a whole. Since that time, this outreach has taken various forms. Many members of the faculty have participated in numerous scholarly conferences, where they have built bridges with professional colleagues. Some have held significant leadership positions in various academic societies or professional organizations. Donald Q. Cannon, for example, was president of the Mormon History Association for 2004–5. A group teaching world religions made an extensive trip to India, China, Korea, and Japan. Dean Millet and other faculty members visited Notre Dame, Catholic University, Wheaton College, and Baylor University to see firsthand how they taught their courses in religion and how academic freedom was viewed on these church-related campuses. Such contacts helped to open channels of communication and mutual respect.

For years Truman G. Madsen had built bridges of understanding through his service in the Richard L. Evans Chair of Christian Understanding. Following his retirement, the chair was divided into two or more professorships with the expectation that the good being done could be spread even more widely.

---

13. "Meeting with General Authorities: New Dean for Religious Education," faculty meeting minutes, January 9, 1991.

Nauvoo became another site for Religious Education's outreach. As Milton Backman, who had taught Church history for many years, served a mission there from 1992 to 1993, he discovered that winter was a definite slack time. Because missionaries were called to serve eighteen

Religious Education faculty and staff, April 17, 1990. (Left to right) **Front row (seated):** *Keith W. Perkins, Paul H. Peterson, S. Kent Brown, Robert L. Millet, Monte S. Nyman, Donald Q. Cannon, Robert J. Matthews, Reed A. Benson, John M. Madsen, Kent P. Jackson.* **Row 2:** *LaMar C. Berrett, Richard L. Anderson, Allyson Brown, Laura Card, Vema Wolfgramm, Susan Easton Black, M. Catherine Thomas, Janiel Lind, Patty A. Smith, Charlotte A. Pollard, Barbara Crawley, Joell Woodbrey, Keith H. Meservy.* **Row 3:** *J. Grant Stevenson, C. Max Caldwell, Paul Y. Hoskisson, Larry C. Porter, E. Dale LeBaron, David F. Boone, Leaun G. Otten, Richard O. Cowan, Roger R. Keller, Bruce A. Van Orden, H. Donl Peterson, Clark V. Johnson, Milton V. Backman Jr., H. Dean Garrett, Byron R. Merrill, George D. Durrant, Stephen E. Robinson, Dennis L. Largey, Robert E. Parsons.* **Row 4:** *Alan K. Parrish, A. Gary Anderson, Victor L. Ludlow, Charles D. Tate Jr., Brent L. Top, George W. Pace, Richard D. Draper, Dong Sull Choi, Leon R. Hartshorn, Walter D. Bowen. Courtesy of Religious Education.*

months from the spring of one year until the fall of the next, several of the fifty historic homes where they lived were vacant during the winter. He therefore suggested giving students an on-site experience in Nauvoo during winter semesters. The program was launched in 1994, and Backman served as its director for the first three years. Although Church history and Doctrine and Covenants classes were at the heart of the curriculum, courses in such subjects as U.S. history and American literature were also included. Classes met in the visitors' center and in various historic buildings around Nauvoo. Field trips visited Church historic sites in New York, Ohio, and Missouri as well as points of general interest like Hannibal, Missouri, and Springfield, Illinois. A weekly community lecture series was open to the public and was typically well attended.

The new adjunct faculty program, launched in 1997, was yet another opportunity for outreach and a means of strengthening relationships across campus. While the former "transfer teachers" were assigned by their departments to fill a quota and often were rotated each semester, the new adjunct instructors taught because they wanted to, generally made a commitment for at least three years, and were regarded as part of the Religious Education faculty. Mingling in faculty meetings and elsewhere strengthened friendships among colleagues who represented a variety of disciplines. University leaders agreed that the adjunct faculty would teach up to one-fourth of all students taking religion, about half would continue to be taught by the full-time Religious Education faculty, and the remaining quarter by visiting personnel from CES or by other selected part-time teachers.

Use of Technology Expanded

During the 1990s, members of the Religious Education faculty made increasing use of computers. A decade earlier, when Keith W. Perkins was chair of the Department of Church History and Doctrine, he obtained Religious Education's first computer to analyze Kirtland tax and land records. At this time computers were used primarily for scientific research, but he wondered why they could not be employed for gospel study as well. He directed department secretaries to begin entering Conference Reports whenever they had free time. Later, key historical works and compilations of Church Presidents' teachings were added to the growing database. Eventually he purchased an optical scanner to accelerate the process. When Milton V. Backman became the RSC director for Church history in 1988, he began entering early Mormon journals into the computer.

Another opportunity for outreach came when Perkins was asked to update his Independent Study course in the Doctrine and Covenants. As he completed this task, he wondered why the course could not be offered over the Internet. When necessary preparations were made and the idea was presented, Continuing Education officials were enthusiastic. The course was offered on a trial basis, one of the first such Internet classes in the nation. Response was great, coming from as far away as Australia and New Zealand. After board review and approval, the course officially went online March 31, 1997. First to register was a forty-seven-year-old student in Japan. The first to complete the class was a Berkeley student who was a member of another faith and asked when other

Religious Education full-time faculty and staff, August 21, 2000. (Left to right) **Front row (kneeling):** *Douglas E. Brinley, E. Dale LeBaron, Reed A. Benson, Thomas A. Wayment, Richard E. Bennett, John P. Livingstone, Fred E. Woods, Frank F. Judd Jr., Richard Neitzel Holzapfel.* **Row 2:** *Gaye Strathearn, Mary Jane Woodger, Byron R. Merrill, Donald Q. Cannon, Ruth Ann Hamilton, Kent P. Jackson, Robert L. Millet, Andrew C. Skinner, Todd B. Parker, Randy L. Bott, Charlotte A. Pollard, Susan Easton Black, Joy Smith, Pat Ward.* **Row 3:** *Patty A. Smith, Connie Lankford, Paul Y. Hoskisson, David F. Boone, Dong Sull Choi, Victor L. Ludlow, Michael D. Rhodes, Brian M. Hauglid, Dennis A. Wright, Camille Fronk, Ray L. Huntington, Barbara Crawley.* **Row 4:** *Linda Godfrey, Lori Soza, Alex L. Baugh, Brent L. Top, Kip Sperry, Rex C. Reeve Jr., Richard D. Draper, Daniel K Judd, Raymond S. Wright, Craig K. Manscill, Larry C. Porter, Clark Thorstenson, Richard O. Cowan.* **Row 5:** *Craig James Ostler, Joseph F. McConkie, S. Kent Brown, Roger R. Keller, Dennis L. Largey, John B. Stohlton, Robert C. Freeman, Arnold K. Garr, Keith J. Wilson, Terry L. Szink, Stanley A. Johnson, Lawrence R. Flake, D. Kelly Ogden.* **Row 6:** *Terry B. Ball, Clyde J. Williams, Vern D. Sommerfeldt, Bruce A. Van Orden, Jerry M. Perkins, Andrew H. Hedges, Clark V. Johnson, Paul H. Peterson, W. Jeffrey Marsh, Matthew O. Richardson. Courtesy of Religious Education.*

religion courses would be available.[14] Religious Education immediately took steps to add other classes. In the year of the pioneer sesquicentennial, Perkins truly was a modern pioneer.

With increased research funds from the university and such tools as computers, a higher share of the faculty became actively involved in scholarly research and writing than ever before. Resulting publications became a growing means of reaching out to yet a broader audience. Even though this scholarship helped improve the quality of teaching, it also brought a modest reduction of one or two classes in the average teacher's class load to allow time for research and writing.

Dean Millet believed that one of the great challenges facing members of the Religious Education faculty was to maintain a wholesome balance between competency as a capable scholar-teacher on one hand and humility as a servant of God on the other. We must "have an eye single to the glory of God," he insisted. "Learn to avoid like a plague the damning influences of arrogance and cynicism." We need to "acknowledge that Christ is the light" and that "we are but dim reflections of that light, at best."[15]

As part of the continuing quest to improve teaching, Religious Education leaders in 1998 established the Religious Education Teaching Fellowship, which would "explore various methods and means for teaching in a religious setting, including research, writing, symposia, and other activities which foster increasing effectiveness in conveying gospel prin-

14. Interview with Keith W. Perkins, March 23, 1998.
15. Robert L. Millet, "'Fools before God': Striking the Delicate Balance between Competence and Humility in a University Setting," message to Religious Education faculty, March 15, 1996.

ciples to students."[16] The first recipients of this fellowship were Matthew O. Richardson and Dennis A. Wright.

About this time, the university began planning to furnish classrooms with a uniform set of equipment to enable teachers to take advantage of the latest technological developments. Religious Education faculty had gained the reputation of being willing to try new methods and programs; many, for example, had embraced Microsoft PowerPoint when it was introduced a few years earlier. University officials therefore consulted with the faculty when developing the new equipment. As a result, during the 2001–2 school year, the Joseph Smith Building was one of the first to receive the new TEC (Technology Enhanced Classroom) facilities. Religious Education led most areas in the extent to which these new facilities were used.

With the advent of the TEC rooms, an increasing number of faculty members gave thought to using digitized images—maps, photographs, or other illustrations—to enhance their teaching. Dennis A. Wright therefore applied for funds to produce a CD with images related to Church history, scripture, and other topics in Religious Education. The Harold B. Lee Library had also been interested in launching such a project, so library officials and Professor Wright moved forward as partners. The result was a growing digital collection of images, numbering in the thousands, as part of the library's home page, available to teachers around the world.

Religious Education also launched its own Web site, which included biographical data on faculty members, a listing of recent faculty

16. "Religious Education Teaching Fellowship," statement provided by Matthew O. Richardson, January 10, 2005.

publications, information about organizations related to Religious Education, a statement of policies, and a catalog of courses. An important feature of the site was an electronic library, which included the scriptures, commentaries, and over a thousand books and articles. Many of these materials were made available by commercial publishers specifically for faculty use.

John P. Livingstone, who was a teaching fellow from 2002 to 2004, developed a Web site designed to help teachers, particularly the adjunct faculty from other departments who were teaching courses in Religious Education. It included electronic audio and visual teaching tools, suggestions for improving teaching, and a list of resources available together with instructions on using TEC rooms and other computer-oriented resources.

The increasing importance of technology was reflected in the 2003 appointment of Richard Crookston as Religious Education's first Technology Services Representative (TSR). Previously, faculty members had been appointed to serve as Computer Services Representatives (CSRs) as part of their regular academic load. Crookston shared Religious Education's vision of its mission and how best to achieve it. At the same time, he worked cooperatively with the Office of Information Technology

Customer Support student personnel stand by to provide needed assistance. Courtesy of Richard B. Crookston.

(OIT) across campus to ensure that religion teachers had the best and latest resources available.

Secretarial Support

Over the years the secretarial pool was another valuable resource for the religion faculty. At first, their almost sole responsibility was typing exams, course materials, and other projects for faculty members. As time went by, they also became responsible for distributing or even preparing printed pictures, slides, tape recordings, and other teaching aids.

David Boone became the supervisor in 1981. In the old Joseph Smith Building, the office was housed in the northeast corner of the basement; the ceiling was so low that utility pipes were wrapped in foam rubber to prevent injury if a person should run into them. There was no room for the audiovisual collections, so they had to be kept in separate rooms. David was also responsible for the faculty library even though it was located in the opposite corner of the building. When the new JSB was being planned, David helped design far more ample, convenient, and efficient facilities for what would become known as the Faculty Support Center. The faculty library would be next door, and the new center would incorporate a storage room for its collections.

When David became a member of the full-time faculty in 1994, he was succeeded as supervisor by Patty Smith, who previously had worked with the Religious Studies Center. Under her leadership, changes were made to further enhance the work of Faculty Support. She and Robert Marks of the Copy Center, directly beneath on the ground floor, proposed connecting their two facilities with a dumbwaiter system. "Rapunzel," as it was nicknamed, ended the necessity of carrying huge stacks of copied materials up the stairs and through the halls. Patty coordinated the involved process of producing student packets for dozens of classes and was also regularly a member of the committees, planning and producing publications for the annual Sperry and Student Symposia; her student workers served as hosts for sessions of these events.

Patty Smith of Faculty Support. Courtesy of Richard B. Crookston.

New technology impacted the center's work. Because faculty members had computers in their offices, they increasingly brought disks with items to be copied for their classes rather than needing them to be typed first. This freed the student workers to help with such other useful projects as transcribing oral interviews or preparing electronic copies of early Church periodicals so they can be searched more quickly. Patty also directed the transfer of slides, videocassettes, and other materials to more compact digital formats, which could be used more efficiently.

Patty Smith and the Faculty Support student staff. Courtesy of Richard B. Crookston.

Annual Student Symposium Started

The idea for the Religious Education Student Symposium was proposed by Richard E. Bennett during the fall of 1998. While attending a seminar for new faculty members, he heard Elder Henry B. Eyring of the Quorum of the Twelve urge BYU to encourage increased learning opportunities for its undergraduate students, even giving them the opportunity to publish material before their graduation. Dr. Bennett, who had coordinated faculty symposia at the University of Manitoba, thought that a symposium for students would be the ideal way to meet this challenge. "Students at Brigham Young University have wonderfully unique views, insights, and interpretations to share concerning the doctrines, history, and modern-day role of The Church of Jesus Christ of Latter-day Saints," Dr. Bennett believed. "Each new generation brings fresh interpretations, perspectives, and viewpoints that deserve to be heard and studied, yet few academic forums exist on this campus for such formal student expression."[17]

The first symposium took place on April 1–2, 1999. Of ninety-nine papers submitted, forty-six were selected for presentation. Seven received cash prizes, and a total of fifteen were published in a two-hundred-page volume. This pattern was repeated in the following years, and by 2008 approximately 250 copies of the proceedings were published annually.

Christopher C. Jones (right) accepts an award from J. Spencer Fluhman, an assistant professor of Church history and doctrine at the 2006 Student Symposium. Courtesy of Richard B. Crookston.

---

17. *Selections from the BYU Religious Education 1999 Student Symposium* (Provo, UT: Brigham Young University, 2000), v.

This symposium provided students with the experience of researching and preparing a scholarly paper, and then presenting it before an audience in a refereed setting. Several found this opportunity so valuable that they submitted papers in one or more subsequent years.

Master's Degree Reinstituted

For several years Dean Millet had discussed with Stanley A. Peterson, CES administrator responsible for seminaries and institutes, whether to offer a master's degree in Religious Education once again. They agreed that the degree should focus on the very topics that seminary instructors were teaching. In addition, Dr. Millet explained, the program should "be rigorous enough to equip those wishing to pursue doctoral training with the necessary skills, and at the same time to provide deeper insights into history and doctrine for those content with a master's degree alone."[18]

Approximately 100 seminary teachers applied to be members of the first group of master's candidates in 2000. Fifteen were selected. After that beginning, similar groups entered the program every two years. Comments from CES administrators as well as from participants have been "almost universally positive." Robert Millet, who has taught courses in New Testament and the Book of Mormon, reflected, "There's nothing quite as enjoyable as having a group as eager to learn and be stretched as persons who teach the restored gospel full time."[19]

18. Robert L. Millet to Richard O. Cowan, November 30, 2004.
19. Millet to Cowan, November 30, 2004.

Continuing Contributions

2000–Present

By the beginning of the twenty-first century, Religious Education had become an important part of the BYU educational experience. Additionally, Religious Education continued to reach out beyond the classroom walls to bless the lives of countless others who could never attend BYU.

Religious Educator Launched

For some time Dean Millet and others had felt the need for creating a journal to provide an additional outlet for the scholarly writings of Religious Education faculty members. At the same time, they hoped it could be a resource to those teaching religion at BYU, in the Church

Educational System, and in the quorums and auxiliaries of the Church. The first edition of the *Religious Educator* appeared in the year 2000.

The editors acknowledged that there were other journals catering to a scholarly Latter-day Saint readership but noted that the *Religious Educator* focused on "teaching the gospel, publishing studies on scripture, doctrine, and LDS Church history, and sharing the messages of outstanding devotional essays."[1]

Millet replaced the temporary editorial board in 2001 with Richard Neitzel Holzapfel, who became the full-time editor in chief. Holzapfel asked Ted D. Stoddard, a writing professor in the Marriott School of Business, to explore design and content issues and prepare guidelines that would enhance the scholarly basis of this new publication. Within a short time, rigorous standards, including a thorough blind peer-review process, were implemented, qualifying the *Religious Educator* as a first-rank scholarly journal.

Holzapfel clarified the purpose of this new venture. "Our hope is to provide readers with carefully prepared, inspirational, and information-packed writings on a wide range of subjects explicitly associated with the Restoration. Teachers, authors, researchers, and students of Latter-day

Courtesy of Richard B. Crookston

1. *Religious Educator* 1 (2000): i.

Saint studies at every level will appreciate discussions of relevant ideas and issues from a perspective of faith."[2]

While only one issue of seven hundred copies was released in 2000, two issues were published the following year. The pattern of publishing three issues per year was established in 2002. By 2008 the circulation had reached 1,700. During the early years, contributors were drawn heavily from the Religious Education faculty at BYU. In the second issue during 2002, however, the editors announced that BYU would "join as partners with CES" to publish some of the outstanding presentations from the annual August CES religious educators' conference.[3]

During this period of development, the *Religious Educator* added a group of non-BYU advisory board members in an effort to ensure that the publication met the needs of its audience beyond the university. The board included Tad R. Callister (Glendale, California), Kathy K. Clayton (Salt Lake City), Milly Day (Indianapolis, Indiana), and Victor L. Walch (Wilsonville, Oregon). Representing Religious Education's commitment to be a blessing to the Church worldwide, not just a BYU audience, this advisory board continues to provide significant review and feedback to the RSC. Fortunately, the *Religious Educator* has been blessed with General Authority contributions, beginning with Elder D. Todd Christofferson's piece "The Faith of a Prophet: Brigham Young's Life and Service."[4] As the audience expanded so did the pool of contributors. About half the articles have come from the BYU faculty, the remainder being contributed by CES personnel and others, including a well-known

---

2. *Religious Educator* 3, no. 2 (2002): vi.
3. *Religious Educator* 2, no. 1 (2001): vi.
4. *Religious Educator* 2, no. 1 (2001): 1–14.

Andrew C. Skinner, dean of Religious Education, 2000–2005. Under Skinner, the increase in faculty writing was met by an increase in publishing venues, one of which was the Religious Educator, *which began producing articles aimed at gospel topics generally and gospel teaching specifically. Photo by Mark Philbrick/BYU.*

non-LDS distinguished professor of history and religious studies at Pennsylvania State University, Philip Jenkins.

Andrew C. Skinner became dean of Religious Education in September 2000. A native of Colorado, he earned his master's degrees in Jewish studies and biblical Hebrew at the Iliff School of Theology and Harvard University, studying also at Hebrew University in Jerusalem. He received his PhD in Near Eastern and European history at the University of Denver. After teaching at Ricks College for four years, he joined the BYU faculty in 1992. He had been serving as chair of the Department of Ancient Scripture for three years when he was appointed as dean.

Publishing Efforts Increased

From the beginning, the Religious Studies Center director was responsible for publication and other business decisions as well as for final editing. To meet the needs of the RSC's expanding publication agenda, R. Devan Jensen joined the staff as executive editor in 2001; he brought significant experience from his editorial work with Deseret Book and the *Ensign*. In the past the RSC had published about two to

In fulfilling the University's focus on mentoring, Religious Education has created many opportunities that allow students to be nurtured and trained through their part time employment on campus. Above, RSC editorial interns benefit from weekly gatherings that focus on the development of skills that will help them not only in their job but in their undergraduate studies. Courtesy of Chase Nebeker.

three books per year, but by 2003 output increased to nine books and three issues of the *RSC Newsletter*.

In 2004 the RSC released a landmark book by Scott H. Faulring, Kent P. Jackson, and Robert J. Matthews, *Joseph Smith's New Translation of the Bible: Original Manuscripts*, a complete transcription of all the changes made in the biblical text by the Prophet, together with explanatory essays.

Also in 2004, Richard D. Draper was appointed an associate dean in Religious Education, leaving a vacancy in the RSC, where Draper had served as director since 2001. Richard Neitzel Holzapfel was asked to take the position as well as to continue as editor in chief of the *Religious Educator* in 2004 until someone could be called take over the journal. A variety of circumstances arose that prevented the appointment of a new editor in chief. As a result, the RSC was reorganized, merging the two positions, RSC director over books and newsletters and editor-in-chief of the *Religious Educator*, into director of publications, overseeing the publication of all RSC products.

Robert J. Matthews examines materials linked with Joseph Smith in his "new translation" of the Bible. Courtesy of Richard B. Crookston.

Highlighting not only the increased publication activity at the RSC but also the continuing effort to raise the quality of publications, the RSC was awarded the Christensen Best Documentary Award at the annual meeting of the Mormon History Association in 2007 for *The Diaries of Charles Ora Card: The Utah Years, 1871–1886* (2006).

New Audiences, New Technology

In 2008, the RSC took steps to increase its presence by creating a Web page specifically dedicated to posting the complete RSC library in English and selections in Spanish and Portuguese, the second and third

most spoken languages in the Church. Also in 2008, the RSC published in English and Spanish a special volume featuring some of the best articles from the first ten years of the *Religious Educator*. These giant steps will ensure the continuing relevance of the research and writing of the Religious Education faculty to the Church at large.

Fundraising Efforts Expanded

Traditionally, most university programs were funded through appropriations from the tithes of the Church. However, as the Church began to grow worldwide, and demands on these sacred funds for needed chapels and temples increased, more emphasis was placed on Brigham Young University and its units seeking to raise more of their own funding. Religious educators, with the assistance of individuals appointed by the university's Development Office, sought to identify potential donors interested in supporting various religion-oriented programs.

These efforts intensified under the leadership of Dean Skinner as evidenced by the 2003 appointment of Ken McCarty as assistant to the dean for development. With his help, Religious Education developed an endowment fund of nearly five million dollars. Proceeds from this endowment have helped to fund the full-time editing position for the RSC and the master's program for CES teachers and U.S. military chaplains. They also have supported the Religious Education Professorship in Moral Education; Brent L. Top was the first to hold this professorship in 2001. Furthermore, funds from the endowment have also provided an additional source of support for Religious Education research projects through what became known as the Dean's Discretionary Fund.

Joy Smith, assistant to the dean, helps with financial needs and other administrative matters. Courtesy of Richard B. Crookston.

From 2004 to 2008, Douglas E. Brinley held the Professorship of Moral Education. His service focused on reminding

Religious Education full-time faculty and staff, September 21, 2006. (Left to right) **Front row:** *R. Devan Jensen, Richard Crookston, Frank F. Judd Jr., Joy Smith, Randy L. Bott, Richard O. Cowan, Arnold K. Garr, Terry B. Ball, Richard D. Draper, John P. Livingstone, Lloyd D. Newell, Kent P. Jackson.* **Row 2:** *Patty A. Smith, Ray L. Huntington, Todd B. Parker, Gaye Strathearn, Andrew C. Skinner, Dong Sull Choi, Kip Sperry, Douglas E. Brinley, Victor L. Ludlow, Jared W. Ludlow, Roger R. Keller.* **Row 3:** *Jeffrey R. Chadwick, Cynthia Doxey, Donald Q. Cannon, Fred E. Woods, Lawrence R. Flake, Michael D. Rhodes, Matthew O. Richardson, Clyde J. Williams, Guy L. Dorius, Mary Jane Woodger, Daniel K Judd, Roger P. Minert, Dennis A. Wright.* **Row 4:** *Robert L. Millet, Kerry M. Muhlestein, Camille Fronk Olson, Byron R. Merrill, S. Kent Brown, John B. Stohlton, Charles L. Swift, Keith J. Wilson, David M. Whitchurch, David F. Boone, Richard E. Bennett, Connie Brace.* **Row 5:** *Dana M. Pike, Allen Ostergar, Dennis L. Largey, Reid L. Neilson, J. Spencer Fluhman, Thomas A. Wayment, Jerry M. Perkins, Alonzo L. Gaskill, Paul H. Peterson, Vern D. Sommerfeldt, Alan K. Parrish, JaLee Clarke.* **Row 6:** *W. Jeffrey Marsh, Joany Pinegar, Linda Godfrey, Stanley A. Johnson, Scott C. Esplin, Robert C. Freeman, Andrew H. Hedges, Alex L. Baugh, Paul Y. Hoskisson, Susan Easton Black.* **Not Pictured:** *Kent R. Brooks, C. Wilfred Griggs, Steven C. Harper, Brian M. Hauglid, Richard Neitzel Holzapfel, Eric D. Huntsman, Craig K. Manscill, D. Kelly Ogden, Craig James Ostler, Stephen E. Robinson, David R. Seely, Terry L. Szink, Brent L. Top, Cheryl Snelgrove, Geneva Pelfrey, Ken McCarty. Photo by Mark Philbrick/BYU.*

the campus community to incorporate honesty and integrity in their professional lives. He organized a symposium in February 2007 cosponsored by Religious Education and the Ira A. Fulton College of Engineering and Technology that was titled "The Gospel: The Foundation for a Professional Career." In the keynote address, Elder Richard G. Scott offered a formula for success in professional life and spoke of the importance of integrity as he and his colleagues pioneered the field of nuclear studies. In 2008 the RSC published the proceedings in a book titled *Moral Foundations: Standing Firm in a World of Shifting Values.*

Annual Easter Conference Inaugurated

In 2003, the Religious Education Administrative Council approved a proposal by Richard Neitzel Holzapfel and Thomas A. Wayment to host a conference on the Saturday before Easter which would focus on the Savior's last twenty-four hours and Resurrection. The conference was held and rebroadcast on KBYU Television, helping Religious Education expand their audience.

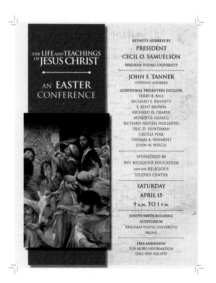

The response to this Easter conference was so positive that the university decided that this should be an annual event held on the day before Easter (Saturday) each year, cosponsored by Religious Education and the RSC. Nearly one thousand attendees heard Elder D. Todd Christofferson give the keynote address at the second annual conference, "The Atonement and the Resurrection," which was later published in the *Religious Educator*.[5] In subsequent years, keynote addresses were delivered by President Cecil O. Samuelson in 2006, Elder F. Enzio Busche in 2007, and President Merrill J. Bateman in 2008. Additionally, the conference provides an opportunity to address current issues about Jesus and the New Testament that seem to surface each Easter season, including *The Da Vinci Code* (2005), the so-called Gospel of Judas (2006), and the Lost Tomb of Jesus (2007).

The BYU Easter Conference has become a permanent feature of Religious Education's efforts to teach the gospel to students and to a much larger audience. In addition to the publication of selections from the conference, BYU-TV and KBYU broadcast the event to an even larger audience today.

Ancient Near Eastern Studies Program Initiated

Following extensive work by a cross-campus committee headed by Dana M. Pike, professor of ancient scripture, university leaders approved a new program allowing students to major or minor in Ancient Near Eastern Studies beginning in 2005. Courses are taught by faculty members from ancient scripture, anthropology, classics, history, and languages. Students can focus either on the Hebrew Old Testament or Greek New Testament. This Bible-centered program encompasses multiple facets of ancient Near Eastern culture. One objective is to provide a rigorous preparation for students going on to challenging graduate work in this field.

---

5.   *Religious Educator* 7, no. 1 (2006): 1–12.

Pike became the first coordinator of this interdepartmental program, and Dean Skinner was named agent dean. This was the first time a dean of Religious Education had administrative stewardship over a program granting undergraduate majors.

Changes at the University Announced

During the fall of 2005, Dean Skinner was invited to become the director of the Institute for the Study and Preservation of Ancient Religious Texts (later renamed the Neal A. Maxwell Institute for Religious Scholarship). Terry B. Ball succeeded him as the dean of Religious Education in 2006. Ball received his bachelor's degree in botany and earned a master's degree in ancient Near Eastern studies. His PhD at BYU in 1992 combined both of these areas, focusing on the archaeobotany of the Near East. He had started his career with CES in 1979, accepting an assignment to teach seminary. He joined the full-time faculty at BYU in 1992, the same year he received his doctorate.

Terry B. Ball, dean of Religious Education, 2006–present. Under Ball's direction, individual professors took on more of the research previously performed through institutions. Religious Education continued to spread its unique offerings beyond the BYU campus through technology, media, and travel study. Courtesy of BYU Photo.

Important changes were taking place at BYU when Ball became dean. The Joseph Fielding Smith Institute for Church History was disbanded in 2005, and many of its members moved to Salt

Lake City to work in the Family and Church History Department (see appendix C).

During that same year, S. Kent Brown, professor of ancient scripture, was named director of the Foundation for Ancient Research and Mormon Studies (FARMS), and in the following year, Ancient Studies (which he had been directing) was formally dissolved. As a result, members of the Religious Education faculty continued the research that had been focused through these other organizations.

Early in 2006, two new research directors were added to the RSC: Richard E. Bennett for Church history and doctrine and Kent P. Jackson for ancient scripture. Both were productive scholars who were widely respected throughout the university and beyond. With increased funding, each director reached out to faculty colleagues to encourage, give direction to, and support worthy research ventures.

BYU Religious Education Review

The RSC began publishing a newsletter in 1986. Former RSC directors S. Kent Brown, Charles D. Tate Jr., Kent P. Jackson, and Richard D. Draper all served as editors in their turn. In 2008 the administrative council approved a proposal to update the newsletter in a brand-new format that would make it possible to "increase exposure to many more facets of Religious Education and of the RSC."[6] The full-color semiannual magazine, christened the *BYU Religious Education Review*, featured articles on the original Joseph Smith Building built in 1941, the teaching

---

6. Richard Neitzel Holzapfel, "A Small Step Forward," *BYU Religious Education Review* 1, no. 1 (2008): 3.

First issue of the BYU Religious Education Review, *March 2008. Previously, important events in Religious Education were announced in a newsletter published triannually. In 2008, a semiannual magazine was launched to bring greater coverage of the developments in Religious Education to a wider audience.*

legacy of Paul H. Peterson (1941–2007), the Saints in World War II Germany, outreach efforts by the Richard L. Evans Chair, RSC internships, and spotlights on donors to Religious Education in the inaugural issue in 2008. The magazine incorporated sections from the old newsletter, such as awards and advancements, interviews with faculty members, a calendar of upcoming events, reports on recent symposia, and new publications. The magazine remains an important vehicle to share news about Religious Education and the RSC.

Contributions Continue

Because most students take a religion class each semester, teachers in Religious Education come in contact with a larger proportion of the student body at a given time than does any other faculty. Religion teachers view this as a great opportunity and solemn responsibility. They are pleased, therefore, that student surveys consistently rank teaching in Religious Education very highly. Various special BYU awards have also reflected the quality of this teaching. Of the first eleven who were named BYU professor of the year, five taught in Religious Education: Daniel H. Ludlow in 1960, Chauncey C. Riddle in 1962, Richard O. Cowan in 1965, Walter D. Bowen in 1966, and Leon R. Hartshorn in 1967. Susan Easton Black was invited to give the annual Karl G. Maeser Distinguished Faculty Lecture in 2000, the most prestigious award given by the university. In 2003, Dr. Cowan was chosen to give the annual Phi Kappa Phi lecture.

Religion faculty members continue to teach beyond their core courses in Religious Education based on their areas of expertise, including classes in the Classics, History, and Marriage, Family, and Human Development departments, and also ancient Near Eastern studies and honors classes. Even in these courses, Religious Education faculty have been acknowledged for their significant contributions. For example, eight faculty members have been recognized as Honors Teacher of the Year: Truman G. Madsen in 1966, Chauncey C. Riddle in 1967, C. Wilfred Griggs in 1975, Richard L. Anderson in 1978, Vern D. Sommerfeldt in 1997,

Professor David R. Seely examines portions of the Dead Sea Scrolls. Courtesy of David R. Seely.

Victor L. Ludlow in 2003, David R. Seely in 2006 (also honored was his wife, Jo Ann, a part-time ancient scripture faculty member who cotaught with David in Honors), and Richard Neitzel Holzapfel in 2008.

Continuing Education is another area where Religious Education makes an important contribution. Evening classes in religion have been among the most in demand. Religious subjects have also been very popular at Education Week. BYU's first Travel Study offering was a Church history tour led by Alma P. Burton in 1951. Two years later, the first tour to the Holy Land was led by Sidney B. Sperry.[7] The first semester in Jerusalem was conducted by Daniel H. Ludlow in 1968, and members of the Religious Education faculty have played a key role there ever since. Several members have also presented radio and television programs.

Like other faculty members in the BYU community, members of the Religious Education faculty have served in a variety of ecclesiastical callings, including bishoprics, stake auxiliary presidencies, stake presidencies, and general board assignments in Salt Lake City. An unusually large number have been called to serve in student stakes and wards. Others have been members of auxiliary general boards or of Churchwide writing and correlation review committees. Twelve were called as mission presidents while serving on the faculty: Ivan J. Barrett, Spencer J. Palmer, Reid E. Bankhead, Truman G. Madsen, Paul R. Cheesman, Walter D. Bowen, Leon R. Hartshorn, Joseph F. McConkie, C. Max Caldwell, H. Dean Garrett, Brent L. Top, and D. Kelly Ogden. In addition, M. Catherine Thomas left to serve with her husband, who was also called as a mission president. Roy W. Doxey was called as a regional representative while serving as college dean. Three faculty members have been called as General Authorities while serving on the faculty: Spencer J. Condie in 1989 and C. Max Caldwell and John M. Madsen in 1992. In 1953, former faculty member Hugh B. Brown was called to be an Assistant to the Twelve, eventually becoming a member of the Quorum of the Twelve and a counselor in the First Presidency. Former dean Jeffrey R. Holland became a member of the Seventy in 1989 and a member of the Quorum of the Twelve Apostles five years later. In 2004,

7. Keith L. Smith, "An Historical Study of Adult Education Programs of the Brigham Young University from 1921 to 1966" (PhD diss., Brigham Young University, 1968), 95–96.

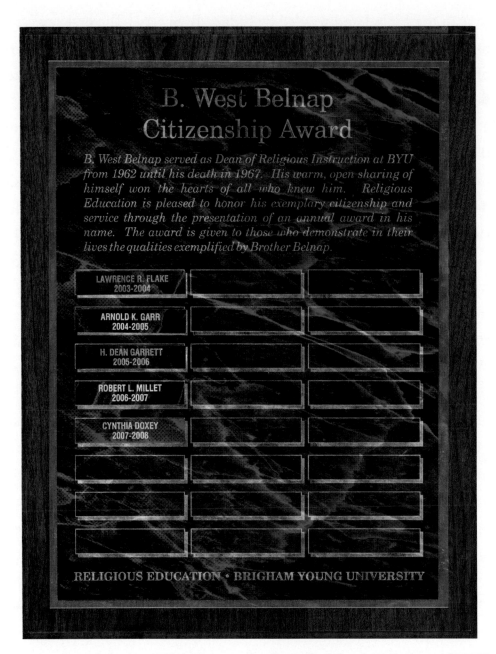

Citizenship, scholarship, and teaching are the three pillars that form the basis of BYU's expectation for every faculty member. Beginning in 1979, Religious Education has honored a faculty member each year with the B. West Belnap Citizenship Award.

Daniel K Judd was called as a counselor in the general Sunday School presidency.

Although everyone recognizes his distinct voice as the announcer of general conferences and *Music and the Spoken Word*, few may know that Lloyd D. Newell is a Religious Education faculty member. Invariably, on the first day of class each semester, when new students recognize his voice, he is required by them to repeat the famous words, "From the crossroads of the West, we welcome you to a program of inspirational music and spoken word," and, "Again we leave you from within the shadow of the everlasting hills. May peace be with you, this day and always."

Daniel K Judd, professor of ancient scripture and first counselor in the general sunday school presidency, speaks at the October 2007 general conference. © Intellectual Reserve.

Continuing Impact of Gospel Scholarship

Religious Education faculty have burned the midnight oil researching, writing, and publishing important contributions to LDS gospel scholarship and beyond. Many Latter-day Saints can find the works of such notable scholars as Richard L. Anderson, Milton V. Backman Jr., LaMar C. Barrett, Kent P. Jackson, Daniel H. Ludlow, Truman G. Madsen, Robert J. Matthews, Robert L. Millet, Hugh W. Nibley, Stephen E. Robinson, and Sidney B. Sperry on their shelves.

Of course, such activity has a greater impact than simply adding to a professor's curriculum vita. Members of the Church and friends

To emphasize the important role of scholarship at the university, Religious Education established the Richard Lloyd Anderson Research Award in 1997.

of other faiths have had questions answered and new vistas opened to them by this important aspect of their university assignment, helping us all to fulfill the Lord's command, "Seek ye out of the best books words of wisdom; seek learning, even by study and also by faith" (Doctrine and Covenants 88:118).

Additionally, involvement in scholarly activity helps faculty members to sharpen and clarify their thinking on the things that matter most. Finally, thoughtful gospel scholarship always infuses a sense of excitement in the classroom as teachers share with their students new insights and discoveries based on solid academic research and writing.

Dr. Thomas A. Wayment (right) of the ancient scripture faculty visits with a student following a New Testament class. Courtesy of Richard B. Crookston.

Robert J. Matthews
Teaching Award

For more than three decades Robert Matthews taught the gospel of Jesus Christ with dignity and persuasion in the classroom and through the written word. His devotion to the Savior and his commitment to the restoration of the fullness of the gospel through the Prophet Joseph Smith have profoundly influenced his students and have raised the level of gospel scholarship throughout the Church. Religious Education is pleased to honor his service through the presentation of an annual award in his name. The award is given annually to those who demonstrate in their teaching the same qualities exemplified by Brother Matthews.

LAMAR E. GARRARD 1991-1992	DANIEL K. JUDD 1999-2000	RICHARD O. COWAN 2007-2008
MONTE S. NYMAN 1992-1993	TODD B. PARKER 2000-2001	
LEAUN G. OTTEN 1993-1994	MATTHEW O. RICHARDSON 2001-2002	
CLYDE J. WILLIAMS 1994-1995	DENNIS L. LARGEY 2002-2003	
DOUGLAS E. BRINLEY 1995-1996	SUSAN EASTON BLACK 2003-2004	
BRENT L. TOP 1996-1997	DONG SULL CHOI 2004-2005	
RAY LYNN HUNTINGTON 1997-1998	BYRON R. MERRILL 2005-2006	
DAVID R. SEELY 1998-1999	PAUL H. PETERSON 2006-2007	

RELIGIOUS EDUCATION • BRIGHAM YOUNG UNIVERSITY

To highlight the fundamental role of teaching at the university, Religious Education honors a faculty member each year who has demonstrated exceptional teaching with the Robert J. Matthews Teaching Award.

Focus on Teaching

Undoubtedly, Religious Education's greatest and longest lasting contribution will be found in the lives of hundreds of thousands of students who sat in the classrooms across campus learning from faculty members.

Faculty members know by personal experience that teaching and learning take place in a variety of settings beyond official class time. This process also occurs just before and after a class ends, during a student consultation in the professor's office in the Joseph Smith Building, in conversations via the telephone and through e-mails. Teaching the word is the heart and soul of Religious Education at BYU.

EPILOGUE

The Future of Religious Education

As we reflect upon the past, we know of the developments and changes that have occurred which have brought us to the present. Although no one knows what new opportunities and challenges lay before Brigham Young University in the twenty-first century, the faculty of Religious Education will certainly continue its efforts to meet the needs of the university and the worldwide Church.

While future developments and changes remain perpetually unknown, two things are certain. As with every branch of the university, Religious Education will continue to fulfill its mission in new ways by creatively adapting to whatever novel circumstances may come. But unique to its role as the hub of the university, Religious Education will always remain an irreplaceable ingredient in the BYU experience, one that gives the university something different and unparalleled to offer the rest of the world. We have not witnessed the sunset, but the sunrise, of Religious Education at BYU.

Appendix A

Excerpts from Foundational Documents

The Charted Course of the Church in Education

President J. Reuben Clark Jr., August 8, 1938

As a school boy I was thrilled with the great debate between those two giants, Webster and Hayne. The beauty of their oratory, the sublimity of Webster's lofty expression of patriotism, the forecast of the civil struggle to come for the mastery of freedom over slavery, all stirred me to the very depths. The debate began over the Foot Resolution concerning the public lands. It developed into consideration of great fundamental problems of constitutional law. I have never forgotten the opening paragraph of Webster's reply, by which he brought back to its place of beginning this debate that had drifted so far from its course. That paragraph reads:

Mr. President: When the mariner has been tossed for many days in thick weather, and on an unknown sea, he naturally avails himself of the first pause in the storm, the earliest glance of the sun, to take his latitude, and ascertain how far the elements have driven him from his true course. Let us imitate this prudence, and, before we float farther on the waves

President J. Reuben Clark Jr. © Intellectual Reserve, Inc.

of this debate, refer to the point from which we departed, that we may at least be able to conjecture where we now are. I ask for the reading of the resolution.

Now I hasten to express the hope that you will not think that I think, this is a Webster-Hayne occasion or that I think I am a Daniel Webster. If you were to think those things—either of them—you would make a grievous mistake. I admit I am old, but I am not that old. But Webster seemed to invoke so sensible a procedure for occasions where, after wandering on the high seas or in the wilderness, effort is to be made to get back to the place of starting, that I thought you would excuse me if I invoked and in a way used this same procedure to restate some of the more outstanding and essential fundamentals underlying our Church school education.

The following are to me those fundamentals:

The Church is the organized priesthood of God, the priesthood can exist without the Church, but the Church cannot exist without the priesthood. The mission of the Church is first, to teach, encourage, assist, and protect the individual member in his striving to live the perfect life, temporally and spiritually, as laid down in the Gospel, "Be ye therefore perfect, even as your Father which is in heaven is perfect," said the Master (Matthew 5:48). Secondly, the Church is to maintain, teach, encourage, and protect, temporally and spiritually, the membership as a group in its living of the gospel. Thirdly, the Church is militantly to proclaim the truth, calling upon all men to repent, and to live in obedience to the gospel, for every knee must bow and every tongue confess (see Mosiah 27:31).

In all this there are for the Church, and for each and all of its members, two prime things which may not be overlooked, forgotten, shaded, or discarded:

First—that Jesus Christ is the Son of God, the Only Begotten of the Father in the flesh, the Creator of the world, the Lamb of God, the Sacrifice for the sins of the world, the Atoner for Adam's transgression; that He was crucified; that His spirit left His body; that He died; that He was laid away in the tomb; that on the third day His spirit was reunited with His body, which again became a living being; that He was raised from the tomb a resurrected being, a perfect Being, the First Fruits of the Resurrection; that He later ascended to the Father; and that because of His death and by and through His resurrection every man born into the world since the beginning will be likewise literally resurrected. This doctrine is as old as the world. Job declared: "And though after my skin worms destroy this body, yet in my flesh shall I see God: Whom I shall see for myself, and mine eyes shall behold, and not another" (Job 19:26–27).

The resurrected body is a body of flesh and bones and spirit, and Job was uttering a great and everlasting truth. These positive facts, and all other facts necessarily implied therein, must all be honestly believed, in full faith, by every member of the Church.

The second of the two things to which we must all give full faith is that the Father and the Son actually and in truth and very deed appeared to the Prophet Joseph in a vision in the woods; that other heavenly visions followed to Joseph and to others; that the gospel and the Holy Priesthood after the Order of the Son of God were in truth and fact restored to the earth from which they were lost by the apostasy of the primitive Church; that the Lord again set up His Church, through the agency of Joseph Smith; that the Book of Mormon is just what it professes to be; that to the Prophet came numerous revelations for the guidance, upbuilding, organization, and encouragement of the Church and its members; that the Prophet's successors, likewise called of God, have received revelations as the needs of the Church have required, and that they will continue to receive revelations as the Church and its members, living the truth they already have, shall stand in need of more; that this is in truth the Church of Jesus Christ of Latter-day Saints; and that its foundation beliefs are the laws and principles laid down in the Articles of Faith. These facts also, and each of them, together with all things necessarily implied therein or flowing therefrom, must stand, unchanged, unmodified, without dilution, excuse, apology, or avoidance; they may not be explained away or submerged. Without these two great beliefs the Church would cease to be the Church.

Any individual who does not accept the fulness of these doctrines as to Jesus of Nazareth or as to the restoration of the gospel and holy priesthood, is not a Latter-day Saint; the hundreds of thousands of faithful, God-fearing men and women who compose the great body of the Church membership do believe these things fully and completely, and they support the Church and its institutions because of this belief.

I have set out these matters because they are the latitude and longitude of the actual location and position of the Church, both in this world and in eternity. Knowing our true position, we can change our bearings if they need changing; we can lay down anew our true course. And here we may wisely recall that Paul said: "But though we, or an angel from heaven, preach any other gospel unto you than that which we have preached unto you, let him be accursed" (Galatians 1:8).

Returning to the Webster-Hayne precedent, I have now finished reading the original resolution.

As I have already said, I am to say something about the religious education of the youth of the Church. I shall bring together what I have to say under two general headings—the student and the teacher. I shall speak very frankly, for we have passed the place where we may wisely talk in ambiguous words and veiled phrases. We must say plainly what we mean, because the future of our youth, both here on earth and in the hereafter, as also the welfare of the whole Church, are at stake.

The youth of the Church, your students, are in great majority sound in thought and in spirit. The problem primarily is to keep them sound, not to convert them.

The youth of the Church are hungry for things of the Spirit; they are eager to learn the gospel, and they want it straight, undiluted. They want to know about the fundamentals I have just set out—about our beliefs; they want to gain testimonies of their truth. They are not now doubters but inquirers, seekers after truth. Doubt must not be planted in their hearts. Great is the burden and the condemnation of any teacher who sows doubt in a trusting soul.

These students crave the faith their fathers and mothers have; they want it in its simplicity and purity. There are few indeed who have not seen the manifestations of its divine power. They wish to be not only the beneficiaries of this faith, but they want to be themselves able to call it forth to work.

They want to believe in the ordinances of the gospel; they wish to understand them so far as they may.

They are prepared to understand the truth, which is as old as the gospel and which was expressed thus by Paul (a master of logic and metaphysics unapproached by the modern critics who decry all religion):

"For what man knoweth the things of a man, save the spirit of man which is in him? even so the things of God knoweth no man, but the Spirit of God. Now we have received, not the spirit of the world, but the spirit which is of God; that we might know the things that are freely given to us of God" (1 Corinthians 2:11–12).

"For they that are after the flesh do mind the things of the flesh; but they that are after the Spirit the things of the Spirit" (Romans 8:5).

"This I say then, Walk in the Spirit, and ye shall not fulfil the lust of the flesh. For the flesh lusteth against the Spirit, and the Spirit against the flesh: and these are contrary the one to the other: so that ye cannot do the things that ye would. But if ye be led of the Spirit, ye are not under the law" (Galatians 5:16–18).

Our youth understand, too, the principle declared in modern revelation:

"Ye cannot behold with your natural eyes, for the present time, the design of your God concerning those things which shall come hereafter, and the glory which shall follow after much tribulation" (D&C 58:3).

"By the power of the Spirit our eyes were opened and our understandings were enlightened, so as to see and understand the things of God. . . . And while we meditated upon these things, the Lord touched the eyes of our understandings and they were opened, and the glory of the Lord shone round about. And we beheld the glory of the Son, on the right hand of the Father, and received of his fulness; And saw the holy angels, and them who are sanctified before his throne, worshiping God, and the Lamb, who worship him forever and ever. And now, after the many testimonies which have been given of him, this is the testimony, last of all, which we give of him: That he lives! For we saw him, even on the right hand of God; and we heard the voice bearing record that he is the Only Begotten of the Father—That by him, and through him, and of him, the worlds are and were created, and the inhabitants thereof are begotten sons and daughters unto God. . . . And while we were yet in the Spirit, the Lord commanded us that we should write the vision" (D&C 76:12, 19–24, 28).

These students are prepared, too, to understand what Moses meant when he declared: "But now mine own eyes have beheld God; but not my natural, but my spiritual eyes, for my natural eyes could not have beheld; for I should have withered and died in his presence; but his glory was upon me; and I beheld his face, for I was transfigured before him" (Moses 1:11).

These students are prepared to believe and understand that all these things are matters of faith, not to be explained or understood by any process of human reason, and probably not by any experiment of known physical science.

These students (to put the matter shortly) are prepared to understand and to believe that there is a natural world and there is a spiritual world; that the things of the natural world will not explain the things of the spiritual world; that the things of the spiritual world cannot be understood or comprehended by the things of the natural world; that you cannot rationalize the things of the Spirit, because first, the things of the Spirit are not sufficiently known and comprehended, and secondly, because finite mind and reason cannot comprehend nor explain infinite wisdom and ultimate truth.

These students already know that they must be "honest, true, chaste, benevolent, virtuous, and [do] good to all men" and that "if there is anything virtuous, lovely, or of good report or praiseworthy, we seek after these things" (Articles of Faith 1:13)—these things they have been taught from very birth. They should be encouraged in all proper ways to do these things which they know to be true, but they do not need to have a year's course of instruction to make them believe and know them.

These students fully sense the hollowness of teachings that would make the gospel plan a mere system of ethics. They know that Christ's teachings are in the highest degree ethical, but they also know they are more than this. They will see that ethics relate primarily to the doings of this life, and that to make of the gospel a mere system of ethics is to confess a lack of faith, if not a disbelief, in the hereafter. They know that the gospel teachings not only touch this life, but the life that is to come, with its salvation and exaltation as the final goal.

These students hunger and thirst, as did their fathers before them, for a testimony of the things of the Spirit and of the hereafter, and knowing that you cannot rationalize eternity, they seek faith and the knowledge which follows faith. They sense, by the Spirit they have, that the testimony they seek is engendered and nurtured by the testimony of others, and that to gain this testimony which they seek for, one living, burning, honest testimony of a righteous God-fearing man that Jesus is the Christ and that Joseph was God's prophet, is worth a thousand books and lectures aimed at debasing the gospel to a system of ethics or seeking to rationalize infinity.

Two thousand years ago the Master said:

"Or what man is there of you, whom if his son ask bread, will he give him a stone? Or if he ask a fish, will he give him a serpent?" (Matthew 7:9–10).

These students, born under the covenant, can understand that age and maturity and intellectual training are not in any way or to any degree necessary to communion with the Lord and His Spirit. They know the story of the youth Samuel in the temple, of Jesus at twelve years confounding the doctors in the temple, of Joseph at fourteen seeing God the

Father and the Son in one of the most glorious visions ever beheld by man. They are not as were the Corinthians, of whom Paul said:

"I have fed you with milk, and not with meat: for hitherto ye were not able to bear it, neither yet now are ye able" (1 Corinthians 3:2).

They are rather as was Paul himself when he declared to the same Corinthians:

"When I was a child, I spake as a child, I understood as a child, I thought as a child: but when I became a man, I put away childish things" (1 Corinthians 13:11).

These students as they come to you are spiritually working on toward a maturity which they will early reach if you but feed them the right food. They come to you possessing spiritual knowledge and experience the world does not know.

So much for your students and what they are and what they expect and what they are capable of. I am telling you the things that some of you teachers have told me, and that many of your youth have told me.

May I now say a few words to you teachers? In the first place, there is neither reason nor is there excuse for our Church religious teaching and training facilities and institutions unless the youth are to be taught and trained in the principles of the gospel, embracing therein the two great elements that Jesus is the Christ and that Joseph was God's prophet. The teaching of a system of ethics to the students is not a sufficient reason for running our seminaries and institutes. The great public school system teaches ethics. The students of seminaries and institutes should of course be taught the ordinary canons of good and righteous living, for these are part, and an essential part, of the gospel. But there are the great principles involved in eternal life, the priesthood, the Resurrection, and many like other things, that go way beyond these canons of good living. These great fundamental principles also must be taught to the youth; they are the things the youth wish first to know about.

The first requisite of a teacher for teaching these principles is a personal testimony of their truth. No amount of learning, no amount of study, and no number of scholastic degrees can take the place of this testimony, which is the *sine qua non* of the teacher in our Church school system. No teacher who does not have a real testimony of the truth of the gospel as revealed to and believed by the Latter-day Saints, and a testimony of the Sonship and Messiahship of Jesus, and of the divine mission of Joseph Smith—including, in all its reality, the First Vision—has any place in the Church school system. If there be any such, and I hope and pray there are none, he should at once resign; if the Commissioner knows of any such and he does not resign, the Commissioner should request his resignation. The First Presidency expect this pruning to be made.

This does not mean that we would cast out such teachers from the Church—not at all. We shall take up with them a labor of love, in all patience and long-suffering, to win them to the knowledge to which as God-fearing men and women they are entitled. But this does mean that our Church schools cannot be manned by unconverted, untestimonied teachers.

But for you teachers the mere possession of a testimony is not enough. You must have, besides this, one of the rarest and most precious of all the many elements of human character—moral courage. For in the absence of moral courage to declare your testimony, it will reach the students only after such dilution as will make it difficult if not impossible for them to detect it; and the spiritual and psychological effect of a weak and vacillating testimony may well be actually harmful instead of helpful.

The successful seminary or institute teacher must also possess another of the rare and valuable elements of character, a twin brother of moral courage and often mistaken for it. I mean intellectual courage— the courage to affirm principles, beliefs, and faith that may not always be considered as harmonizing with such knowledge, scientific or otherwise, as the teacher or his educational colleagues may believe they possess.

Not unknown are cases where men of presumed faith, holding responsible positions, have felt that, since by affirming their full faith they might call down upon themselves the ridicule of their unbeliev- ing colleagues, they must either modify or explain away their faith, or destructively dilute it, or even pretend to cast it away. Such are hypo- crites to their colleagues and to their co-religionists.

An object of pity (not of scorn, as some would have it) is that man or woman who, having the truth and knowing it, finds it necessary either to repudiate the truth or to compromise with error in order that he may live with or among unbelievers without subjecting himself to their disfa- vor or derision as he supposes. Tragic indeed is his place, for the real fact is that all such discardings and shadings in the end bring the very pun- ishments that the weak-willed one sought to avoid. For there is nothing the world so values and reveres as the man who, having righteous con- victions, stands for them in any and all circumstances; there is nothing toward which the world turns more contempt than the man who, hav- ing righteous convictions, either slips away from them, abandons them, or repudiates them. For any Latter-day Saint psychologist, chemist, physicist, geologist, archeologist, or any other scientist, to explain away, or misinterpret, or evade or elude, or most of all, to repudiate or to deny the great fundamental doctrines of the Church in which he professes to believe, is to give the lie to his intellect, to lose his self-respect, to bring sorrow to his friends, to break the hearts and bring shame to his parents, to besmirch the Church and its members, and to forfeit the respect and honor of those whom he has sought, by his course, to win as friends and helpers.

I prayerfully hope there may not be any such among the teachers of the Church school system, but if there are any such, high or low, they must travel the same route as the teacher without the testimony. Sham and pretext and evasion and hypocrisy have, and can have, no place in the Church school system or in the character building and spiritual growth of our youth.

Another thing that must be watched in our Church institutions is this: It must not be possible for men to keep positions of spiritual trust who, not being converted themselves, being really unbelievers, seek to turn aside the beliefs, education, and activities of our youth, and our aged also, from the ways they should follow into other paths of education, beliefs, and activities which (though leading where the unbeliever would go) do not bring us to places where the gospel would take us. That this works as a conscience-balm to the unbeliever who directs it is of no importance. This is the grossest betrayal of trust; and there is too much reason to think it has happened.

I wish to mention another thing that has happened in other lines, as a caution against the same thing happening in the Church Educational System. On more than one occasion our Church members have gone to other places for special training in particular lines. They have had the training which was supposedly the last word, the most modern view, the *ne plus ultra* of up-to-dateness; then they have brought it back and dosed it upon us without any thought as to whether we needed it or not. I refrain from mentioning well-known and, I believe, well-recognized instances of this sort of thing. I do not wish to wound any feelings.

But before trying on the newest fangled ideas in any line of thought, education, activity, or what not, experts should just stop and consider that however backward they think we are, and however backward we may actually be in some things, in other things we are far out in the lead, and therefore these new methods may be old, if not worn out, with us.

In whatever relates to community life and activity in general, to clean group social amusement and entertainment, to closely knit and carefully directed religious worship and activity, to a positive, clear-cut, faith-promoting spirituality, to a real, everyday, practical religion, to a firm-fixed desire and acutely sensed need for faith in God, we are far in the van of on-marching humanity. Before effort is made to inoculate us with new ideas, experts should kindly consider whether the methods used to spur community spirit or build religious activities among groups that are decadent and maybe dead to these things are quite applicable to us, and whether their effort to impose these upon us is not a rather crude, even gross anachronism.

For example, to apply to our spiritually minded and religiously alert youth a plan evolved to teach religion to youth having no interest or concern in matters of the Spirit would not only fail in meeting our actual religious needs, but would tend to destroy the best qualities which our youth now possess.

I have already indicated that our youth are not children spiritually; they are well on toward the normal spiritual maturity of the world. To treat them as children spiritually, as the world might treat the same age group, is therefore and likewise an anachronism. I say once more, there is scarcely a youth that comes through your seminary or institute door who has not been the conscious beneficiary of spiritual blessings, or who has not seen the efficacy of prayer, or who has not witnessed the power of faith to heal the sick, or who has not beheld spiritual outpourings of which the world at large is today ignorant. You do not have to sneak up behind this spiritually experienced youth and whisper religion in his ears; you can come right out, face to face, and talk with him. You do not need to disguise religious truths with a cloak of worldly things; you can bring these truths to him openly, in their natural guise. Youth may prove to be not more fearful of them than you are. There is no need for gradual approaches, for "bedtime" stories, for coddling, for patronizing, or for any of the other childish devices used in efforts to reach those spiritually inexperienced and all but spiritually dead.

You teachers have a great mission. As teachers you stand upon the highest peak in education, for what teaching can compare in priceless value and in far-reaching effect with that which deals with man as he was in the eternity of yesterday, as he is in the mortality of today, and as he will be in the forever of tomorrow. Not only time but eternity is your field. Salvation of yourself not only, but of those who come within the purlieus of your temple is the blessing you seek, and which, doing your duty, you will gain. How brilliant will be your crown of glory, with each soul saved an encrusted jewel thereon.

But to get this blessing and to be so crowned, you must, I say once more, you must teach the gospel. You have no other function and no other reason for your presence in a Church school system.

You do have an interest in matters purely cultural and in matters of purely secular knowledge, but, I repeat again for emphasis, your chief interest, your essential and all but sole duty, is to teach the gospel of the Lord Jesus Christ as that has been revealed in these latter days. You are to teach this gospel, using as your sources and authorities the standard works of the Church and the words of those whom God has called to lead His people in these last days. You are not, whether high or low, to intrude into your work your own peculiar philosophy, no matter what its source or how pleasing or rational it seems to you to be. To do so would be to have as many different churches as we have seminaries—and that is chaos.

You are not, whether high or low, to change the doctrines of the Church or to modify them as they are declared by and in the standard works of the Church and by those whose authority it is to declare the mind and will of the Lord to the Church. The Lord has declared that he is "the same yesterday, today, and forever" (2 Nephi 27:23).

I urge you not to fall into that childish error, so common now, of believing that merely because man has gone so far in harnessing the forces of nature and turning them to his own use that therefore the truths of the Spirit have been changed or transformed. It is a vital and significant fact that man's conquest of the things of the Spirit has not marched side by side with his conquest of things material. The opposite sometimes seems to be true. Man's power to reason has not matched his power to figure. Remember always and cherish the great truth of the Intercessory Prayer:

"And this is life eternal, that they might know thee the only true God, and Jesus Christ, whom thou hast sent" (John 17:3).

This is an ultimate truth; so are all spiritual truths. They are not changed by the discovery of a new element, a new ethereal wave, nor by clipping off a few seconds, minutes, or hours of a speed record.

You are not to teach the philosophies of the world, ancient or modern, pagan or Christian, for this is the field of the public schools. Your sole field is the gospel, and that is boundless in its own sphere.

We pay taxes to support those state institutions whose function and work it is to teach the arts, the sciences, literature, history, the languages, and so on through the whole secular curriculum. These institutions are to do this work. But we use the tithes of the Church to carry on the Church school system, and these are impressed with a holy trust. The Church seminaries and institutes are to teach the gospel.

In thus stating this function time and time again, and with such continued insistence as I have done, it is fully appreciated that carrying out the function may involve the matter of "released time" for our seminaries and institutes. But our course is clear. If we cannot teach the gospel, the doctrines of the Church, and the standard works of the Church, all of them, on "released time" in our seminaries and institutes, then we must face giving up "released time" and try to work out some other plan of carrying on the gospel work in those institutions. If to work out some other plan be impossible, we shall face the abandonment of the seminaries and institutes and the return to Church colleges and academies.

We are not now sure, in the light of developments, that these should ever have been given up.

We are clear upon this point, namely, that we shall not feel justified in appropriating one further tithing dollar to the upkeep of our seminaries and institutes of religion unless they can be used to teach the gospel in the manner prescribed. The tithing represents too much toil, too much self-denial, too much sacrifice, too much faith, to be used for the colorless instruction of the youth of the Church in elementary ethics. This decision and situation must be faced when the next budget is considered. In saying this, I am speaking for the First Presidency.

All that has been said regarding the character of religious teaching, and the results which in the very nature of things must follow a failure properly to teach the gospel, applies with full and equal force to seminaries, to institutes, and to any and every other educational institution belonging to the Church school system.

The First Presidency earnestly solicit the wholehearted help and cooperation of all you men and women who, from your work on the firing line, know so well the greatness of the problem that faces us and which so vitally and intimately affects the spiritual health and the salvation of our youth, as also the future welfare of the whole Church. We need you; the Church needs you; the Lord needs you. Restrain not yourselves, nor withhold your helping hand.

In closing, I wish to pay a humble but sincere tribute to teachers. Having worked my own way through school—high school, college, and professional school—I know something of the hardship and sacrifice this demands; but I know also the growth and satisfaction that come as we reach the end. So I stand here with a knowledge of how many, perhaps most of you, have come to your present place. Furthermore, for a time I tried, without much success, to teach school, so I know also the feelings of those of us teachers who do not make the first grade and must rest in the lower ones.

I know the present amount of actual compensation you get and how very sparse it is—far, far too sparse. I wish from the bottom of my heart we could make it greater; but the drain on the Church income is already so great for education that I must in honesty say there is no immediate prospect for betterment. Our budget for this school year is $860,000, or almost 17 percent of the estimated total cost of running the whole Church, including general administration, stakes, wards, branches, and mission expenses, for all purposes, including welfare and charities. Indeed, I wish I felt sure that the prosperity of the people would be so ample that they could and would certainly pay tithes enough to keep us going as we are.

So I pay my tribute to your industry, your loyalty, your sacrifice, your willing eagerness for service in the cause of truth, your faith in God and in His work, and your earnest desire to do the things that our ordained leader and prophet would have you do. And I entreat you not to make the mistake of thrusting aside your leader's counsel, or of failing to carry out his wish, or of refusing to follow his direction. David of old, privily cutting off only the skirt of Saul's robe, uttered the cry of a smitten heart:

"The Lord forbid that I should do this thing unto my master, the Lord's anointed, to stretch forth mine hand against him, seeing he is the anointed of the Lord" (1 Samuel 24:6).

May God bless you always in all your righteous endeavors. May He quicken your understanding, increase your wisdom, enlighten you by experience, bestow upon you patience, charity, and, as among your most precious gifts, endow you with the discernment of spirits that you may certainly know the spirit of righteousness and its opposite as they come to you. May He give you entrance to the hearts of those you teach and then make you know that as you enter there you stand in holy places that must be neither polluted nor defiled, either by false or corrupting doctrine or by sinful misdeed. May He enrich your knowledge with the skill and power to teach righteousness. May your faith and your testimonies increase, and your ability to encourage and foster them in others grow greater every day—all that the youth of Zion may be taught, built up, encouraged, heartened, that they may not fall by the wayside, but go on to eternal life, that these blessings coming to them, you through them may be blessed also. And I pray all this in the name of Him who died that we might live, the Son of God, the Redeemer of the world, Jesus Christ, amen.

THE SECOND CENTURY
OF BRIGHAM YOUNG UNIVERSITY

President Spencer W. Kimball, October 10, 1975

Brigham Young University [should become] an "educational Everest." There are many ways in which BYU can tower above other universities— not simply because of the size of its student body or its beautiful campus—but because of the unique light BYU can send forth into the educational world. Your light must have a special glow, for while you will do many things in the programs of this University that are done elsewhere, these same things can and must be done better here than others do them. You will also do some special things here that are left undone by other institutions.

President Spencer W. Kimball. © Intellectual Reserve, Inc.

First among these unique features is the fact that dedication on this campus deliberately and persistently concerns itself with "education for eternity," not just for time. The faculty has a double heritage which they must pass along: the secular knowledge that history has washed to the feet of mankind with the new knowledge brought by scholarly research—but also the vital and revealed truths that have been sent to us from heaven. . . .

BYU is being made even more unique, not because what we are doing is changing, but because of the general abandonment by other universities of their efforts to lift the daily behavior and morality of their students. . . . We have no choice at BYU except to "hold the line" regarding gospel standards and values. . . .

When the pressures mount for us to follow the false ways of the world, we hope in the years yet future that those who are part of this University and the Church Educational System will not attempt to counsel the Board of Trustees to follow false ways. We want, through your administration, to receive all your suggestions for making BYU even better. I hope none will presume on the prerogatives of the prophets of God to set the basic direction for this University.

While the discovery of new knowledge must increase, there must always be a heavy and primary emphasis on transmitting knowledge—on the quality of teaching at BYU. Quality teaching is a tradition never to be abandoned. It includes a quality relationship between faculty and students. . . . "Whatever you do, be choice in your selection of teachers," stressed President John Taylor. "We do not want infidels to mould the minds of our children. . . . I would rather have my children taught the simple rudiments of a common education by men of God, and have them under their influence, than have them taught in the most abstruse sciences by men who have not the fear of God in their hearts . . ." (*Journal of Discourses*, 24:168–69).

We [must] continue, in the second century, to be concerned about the spiritual qualities and abilities of those who teach here. In the book of Mosiah we read, ". . . trust no one to be your teacher nor your minister, except he be a man of God, walking in his ways and keeping his commandments" (23:14).

As previous First Presidencies have said, and we say again to you, we expect (we do not simply hope) that Brigham Young University will "become a leader among the great universities of the world." To that expectation I would add, "Become a unique university in all of the world!"

The Gospel Teacher and His Message

President Ezra Taft Benson, September 17, 1976

I am sure you appreciate the fact that you have been given custody of some of the choicest spirits of all time. I emphasize that. These are not just ordinary spirits, but among them are some of the choicest spirits that have come from heaven. These are they who were reserved to come forth in this time to bear off the kingdom triumphant.

This evening I desire to speak on the subject "The Gospel Teacher and His Message." In doing so, I speak not only to the teacher who spends time in the classroom, but I speak also to you partners, for you are a teaching team. Unless you

President Ezra Taft Benson. © Intellectual Reserve, Inc.

and your mate are united in purpose, dedication, and loyalty, you will not succeed to the extent you otherwise could.

Prepare Yourself Spiritually

... All of you were interviewed by a General Authority when you applied for employment in the Church Educational System. I assume most of you were asked if you possessed a testimony—that personal

witness—of Joseph Smith's calling and of the divinity of Jesus Christ.
. . . We assume that every one of you, without any equivocation, has such
a testimony; otherwise, you are flying under false colors and your teaching is a sham—a pretense. . . .

Before you can strengthen your students, it is essential that you study
the doctrines of the kingdom and learn the gospel by *both* study and faith. To
study by faith is to seek understanding and the Spirit of the Lord through
the prayer of faith. Then you will have the power to convince your students.
This is not just good advice; it is a commandment of the Lord [see D&C
88:77, 78; 42:14; 11:21]. . . . The sequence to possessing the power of God
in your teaching is to seek first to obtain the word; then comes understanding and the Spirit, and finally the power to convince. . . .

Always remember, there is no satisfactory substitute for the scriptures
and the words of the living prophets. These should be your original sources.
Read and ponder more what the Lord has said, and less about what others
have written concerning what the Lord has said.

I would hope that each morning before you leave your homes you kneel
before the Lord in secret as well as family prayer. I also hope that before you
go into the classroom you ask to be led by the Spirit. The most important
part of your teaching preparation is that you are guided by the Spirit.

Teach Only the Gospel of Jesus Christ

. . . In 1938 President J. Reuben Clark, Jr., speaking for the First Presidency, pronounced a charge to you in an address entitled "The Charted
Course of the Church in Education." All of you should have a copy of this
address and read it at least at the beginning of each teaching year. . . .

More recently, President Harold B. Lee renewed this charge in these words: "You're to teach the old doctrines, not so plain that they can just understand, *but you must teach the doctrines of the Church so plainly that no one can misunderstand*" ("Loyalty," address to seminary and institute personnel, July 8, 1966, 9; emphasis added). As you stay with the fundamental doctrines and gospel principles, adhering to the standard works, the words of the Brethren, and your Church Educational System outlined courses of study, seeking the guidance of the Spirit, you should have no trouble following this counsel....

Some of our teachers have said, "I can see how the counsel to teach the gospel of Jesus Christ is applicable to gospel subjects, but what about subjects such as Church history that deal in facts?" I would answer this by saying that facts should be taught not only as facts; they should be taught to increase one's faith in the gospel, to build testimony.... Should you wonder how this is done, carefully study the Book of Mormon to see how Mormon did it with his "and thus we see" passages....

Doctrinal interpretation is the province of the First Presidency. The Lord has given that stewardship to them by revelation. No teacher has the right to interpret doctrine for the members of the Church.

Live As You Teach

...Be consistent in your life with the message you declare to your students. The majority of you have provided strong, commendable examples of what a Latter-day Saint life and home should be. How many students have been induced into righteous decisions because of the examples of their seminary and institute teachers!...

President Harold B. Lee made memorable this expression: "If you want to lift another soul, you yourself must be standing on higher ground." That "higher ground" is your persuasive example in keeping the commandments. . . .

I witness to you that God lives. He hears and answers prayers. Jesus is the Christ, the Redeemer of the world and Advocate with the Father. These two heavenly beings did in very deed appear to Joseph Smith—the greatest event that has occurred in this world since the resurrection of Jesus Christ.

I witness that this is the Lord's Church, even The Church of Jesus Christ of Latter-day Saints. He presides over it and is close to his servants. He is not an absentee Master; of that you can be assured.

I witness to you that President Spencer W. Kimball is His living prophet. I love and sustain him with all my soul. Listen to his messages, for that is what the Lord would have you understand for our day and time.

God bless you. I pray the Lord's blessings on you and your families. May you be ever faithful and true to the great trust the Lord and his First Presidency have reposed in you to uphold, sustain, and defend the faith. In the name of Jesus Christ, amen.

THE MANTLE IS FAR, FAR GREATER THAN THE INTELLECT

President Boyd K. Packer, August 1981

The fact that I speak quite directly on a most important subject will, I hope, be regarded as something of a tribute to you who are our loyal, devoted, and inspired associates.

I have come to believe that it is the tendency for many members of the Church who spend a great deal of time in academic research to begin to judge the Church, its doctrine, organization, and leadership, present and past, by the principles of their own profession. Ofttimes this is done unwittingly, and some of it, perhaps, is not harmful.

President Boyd K. Packer. © Intellectual Reserve, Inc.

It is an easy thing for a man with extensive academic training to measure the Church using the principles he has been taught in his professional training as his standard. In my mind it ought to be the other way around. A member of the Church ought always, particularly if he is pursuing extensive academic studies, to judge the professions of man against the revealed word of the Lord. . . .

You seminary teachers and some of you institute and BYU men will be teaching the history of the Church this school year. This is an unparalleled opportunity in the lives of your students to increase their faith and testimony of the divinity of this work. Your objective should be that they will see the hand of the Lord in every hour and every moment of the Church from its beginning till now.

As one who has taken the journey a number of times, I offer four cautions before you begin.

First Caution

There is no such thing as an accurate, objective history of the Church without consideration of the spiritual powers that attend this work. . . . If anything, we are more vulnerable than those in some other disciplines. Church history can be so interesting and so inspiring as to be a very powerful tool indeed for building faith. If not properly written or properly taught, it may be a faith destroyer. . . . If we who research, write, and teach the history of the Church ignore the spiritual on the pretext that the world may not understand it, our work will not be objective. . . . We would end up with a history with the one most essential ingredient left out. . . .

Second Caution

There is a temptation for the writer or the teacher of Church history to want to tell everything, whether it is worthy or faith promoting or not. . . . Teaching some things that are true, prematurely or at the wrong time, can invite sorrow and heartbreak instead of the joy intended to accompany learning. . . . It matters very much not only *what* we are told but *when* we are told it. Be careful that you build faith rather than destroy it . . . . One who chooses to follow the tenets of his profession, regardless of how they may injure the Church or destroy the faith of those not ready for "advanced history," is himself in spiritual jeopardy. If that one is a member of the Church, he has broken his covenants and will be accountable. . . .

Third Caution

In an effort to be objective, impartial, and scholarly, a writer or a teacher may unwittingly be giving equal time to the adversary. . . . In the Church we are not neutral. We are one-sided. There is a war going on, and we are engaged in it. It is the war between good and evil, and we are belligerents defending the good. We are therefore obliged to give preference to and protect all that is represented in the gospel of Jesus Christ. . . . Those of you who are employed by the Church have a special responsibility to build faith, not destroy it. If you do not do that, but in fact accommodate the enemy, who is the destroyer of faith, you become in that sense a traitor to the cause you have made covenants to protect. . . . We should not be ashamed to be committed, to be converted, to be biased in favor of the Lord. . . .

Fourth Caution

The final caution concerns the idea that so long as something is already in print, so long as it is available from another source, there is nothing out of order in using it in writing or speaking or teaching. Surely you can see the fallacy in that. . . . Moroni gave an excellent rule for historians to follow [see Moroni 7:16–17].

Those are the cautions I give to you who teach and write Church history....

The Brethren then and now are men, very ordinary men, who have come for the most part from very humble beginnings. We need your help! We desperately need it. We cannot research and organize the history of the Church. We do not have the time to do it. And we do not have the training that you possess. But we do know the Spirit and how essential a part of our history it is....

May God bless you who so faithfully compile and teach the history of the Church and build the faith of those you teach. I bear witness that the gospel is true. The Church is His church. I pray that you may be inspired as you write and as you teach. May His Spirit be with you in rich abundance.

As you take your students over the trails of Church history in this dispensation, yours is the privilege to help them to see the miracle of the Restoration, the mantle that belongs to His servants, and to "see in every hour and in every moment of the existence of the Church . . . the overruling, almighty hand of [God]" (Joseph F. Smith, in Conference Report, April 1904, 2).

As you write and as you teach Church history under the influence of His Spirit, one day you will come to know that you were not only spectators but a central part of it, for you are His Saints.

This testimony I leave, with my blessings, in the name of Jesus Christ, amen.

"Seek Learning, Even by Study and Also by Faith"

President Boyd K. Packer, April 1974

What I shall attempt to do is to pinpoint a feature or two against the background history of religious education at Brigham Young University and in the Church. You should already be familiar with that history, and we can give it little attention, save to spotlight a place or two where we may have stubbed our toe, where we have tripped and almost stumbled. If we are wise we will step over such places in the future. . . .

In 1954, all the seminary and institute teachers (by this time a goodly number) were assembled for the first time in many years for a Summer School of intensive instruction. The Brethren sent a teacher, Elder Harold B. Lee, of the Council of the Twelve Apostles. . . . There was good reason to check the moorings. For there had grown up among many teachers the feeling that the teaching of basic principles of the gospel might somehow be left perhaps to the Sunday School. These few teachers felt there were more interesting things to do in their classes. They would explore some of the side roads, those that had not received attention in Sunday School or from the Brethren.

They seemed to feel that a testimony would come automatically to their students. Perhaps by accretion the environment would satisfy that need, and they would add the unusual things that they had discovered in their academic wandering. Some took their students with them on these academic excursions, and many of them were lost.

Follow the Brethren

... When I was appointed as supervisor of seminaries.... [we] spent no small part of our time trying to satisfy the inquiries of General Authorities who had been to conferences throughout the Church and had received complaints that some students, while studying religion at Church schools, had lost their testimonies. On one significant occasion, ... we spent the day wrestling with the problems of our seminary and institute teachers. ... The exertions of that day brought us three simple words: Follow the Brethren. This became our motto....

"Division of Religion"

At about that time I had my first close association with the teachers of religion at Brigham Young University. In those days they labored under a designation that unfortunately was only too descriptive, the "Division of Religion."

They were not only divided among themselves, but from the faculties of the other disciplines at the University. They were divided from their brethren in the seminaries and institutes of religion, compatriots who, like themselves, had chosen to devote themselves to the occupation of teaching the gospel of Jesus Christ in the classroom. Some of them were divided in lengthy philosophical contests, for the most part over what mix there would be in the learning "by study" and also "by faith." ...

In the Division of Religion, the brethren wanted, and naturally so, a place in the sun. . . . [So] in January of 1959, the College of Religious Instruction was organized, . . . [but it] has now been dissolved; for that too, by the very title, tended to isolate you from the other faculties, who sometimes assumed that they had little responsibility for the spiritual development of their students. . . .

So here we are. We find ourselves on course. . . .

May I counsel you as to where you might stumble. First, avoid the tendency to feed meat when milk would suffice. Surely that reference needs no explanation to you.

Next, there may be the tendency for you to teach without talent and inspiration because you have a captive audience. Every student at the University is obliged to take religion courses during every semester that he is in residence. No student will be penalized by this rule unless you take advantage of it and become lazy.

Next, many of you are specialists, and you ought to continue to specialize. But please know that however specialized you become in one thing, you must remain expert in several others. For instance, if you are a specialist in the archaeology of the Old Testament, there is not the slightest excuse for you to be deficient as a teacher of the Book of Mormon or of the Doctrine and Covenants or of the New Testament. If you are assigned to teach these areas to undergraduates and feel that you are being misused because you are a specialist, you need to repent. If you have a tendency to set aside these things, you are drifting from what it is all about.

The adulation of the young can easily be misunderstood and misused. If you are a talented teacher, you may have the tendency to be as foolish as the missionary who draws a convert, not to the gospel and the Church, but to himself. I caution you vigorously about that.

I add the tendency to be diverted from your teachings to do research and writing. Now, that may sound strange to you, but it seems to me that writing and research are, in true perspective, subsidiary to teaching. Both can make teaching more effective. Each has a proper place. I do not say ignore them; I say "do not be diverted by them." . . .

Finally, I speak of pedagogical hobbies. A teacher may see something to which others may not be paying adequate attention. He may appoint himself to see that it is not neglected, and then overdo it. Almost anything can be overemphasized, as well as neglected. We have examples of that in religious education as it relates to economics or politics, to patterns of Church government, even to the priesthood. I advise you to be careful and remember this Book of Mormon definition:

"Priestcrafts are that men preach and set themselves up for a light unto the world, that they may get gain and praise of the world; but they seek not the welfare of Zion" (2 Nephi 26:29).

Administrative and Other Officers

The Division of Religion (1939–59)

Director of Religious Activities

    1939–47   J. Wyley Sessions

    1948–49   Hugh B. Brown

Director of Religious Instruction

    1947–53   Sidney B. Sperry

Director of the Undergraduate Division of Religion

    1953–58   B. West Belnap

    1958–59   David H. Yarn Jr.

Director of Graduate Studies

    1953–59   Sidney B. Sperry

College of Religious Instruction (1959–73)
Religious Instruction (1973–83)
Religious Education (1983–present)

Deans

1959–62	David H. Yarn Jr.
1962–66	B. West Belnap
1966–67	Roy W. Doxey (acting)
1967–70	Daniel H. Ludlow
1970–71	Roy W. Doxey (acting)
1971–74	Roy W. Doxey
1974–76	Jeffrey R. Holland
1976–81	Ellis T. Rasmussen
1981–90	Robert J. Matthews
1990–91	Donald Q. Cannon (acting)
1991–2000	Robert L. Millet
2000–2005	Andrew C. Skinner
2006–	Terry B. Ball

Assistant Deans

1969–71	Roy W. Doxey
1971–76	Ellis T. Rasmussen

Associate Deans

1982–91	Monte S. Nyman
1986–90	Donald Q. Cannon

1991–97	Donald Q. Cannon
1991–97	Larry E. Dahl
1997–2002	Paul Y. Hoskisson
1997–2002	Brent L. Top
2002–4	Terry B. Ball
2002–6	Matthew O. Richardson
2004–7	Richard D. Draper
2006–	Dennis A. Wright
2007–	Kent P. Jackson

Assistants to the Dean
Formerly administrative assistants

1973–76	Evelyn Scheiss
1976–86	Rene Mortenson
1986–	Joy L. Smith

Department Chairs

Bible and Modern Scripture

1940–54	Sidney B. Sperry
1954–58	Roy W. Doxey
1958–59	Eldin Ricks
1959–61	Daniel H Ludlow
1961–62	Howard H. Barron

Biblical Languages

1959–60	Sidney B. Sperry
1960–62	Ellis T. Rasmussen

Church Organization and Administration
Renamed LDS Organization and Administration in 1955

1940–48	Wesley P. Lloyd
1948–49	Hugh B. Brown
1949–51	————————
1951–52	Sidney B. Sperry (acting)
1952–53	B. West Belnap (acting)
1953–54	B. West Belnap
1954–57	Chauncey C. Riddle
1957–59	G. Byron Done

Theology and Religious Philosophy
Renamed Theology and Philosophy in 1955

1940–47	J. Wyley Sessions
1948–50	Sidney B. Sperry (acting)
1950–51	————————
1951–57	David H. Yarn Jr.
1957–58	Chauncey C. Riddle
1958–59	Truman G. Madsen

Church History
Renamed LDS Church History in 1955

1940–46	Russell Swensen
1946–48	————————
1948–54	Hugh Nibley
1954–56	Russell R. Rich (acting)
1956–59	Russell R. Rich

LDS Theology, Church Organization and Administration
Renamed Theology and Church Administration in 1960

1959–60	G. Byron Done
1960–62	Rodney Turner

History and Philosophy of Religion

1959–62	Truman G. Madsen

Religious Education

1959–61	B. West Belnap
1961–62	Chauncey C. Riddle

Undergraduate Studies in Religion

1963–69	Roy W. Doxey

Graduate Studies in Religion

1963–69	Chauncey C. Riddle (graduate dean—March 1969)

Ancient Scripture

1969–71	Ellis T. Rasmussen
1971–75	Robert C. Patch
1973–74	Monte S. Nyman (acting)
1975–81	Robert J. Matthews
1981–82	Monte S. Nyman (acting)
1982–85	S. Kent Brown
1985–88	George A. Horton Jr.
1988–91	Robert L. Millet
1991–97	Stephen E. Robinson
1997–2000	Andrew C. Skinner
2000–2004	Daniel K Judd
2004–5	Terry B. Ball

2006–   Dennis L. Largey

Church History and Doctrine

1969–75   LaMar C. Berrett

1975–82   Larry C. Porter

1982–89   Keith W. Perkins

1989–91   Larry E. Dahl

1991–94   Leon R. Hartshorn

1994–97   Richard O. Cowan

1997–2000   Raymond S. Wright

2000–2006   Paul H. Peterson

2006–   Arnold K. Garr

Philosophy
Transferred to the College of General Studies in 1972

1962–66   James R. Clark

1966–69   Chauncey C. Riddle

1969–71   C. Terry Warner

1971–72   Noel B. Reynolds

Associate Department Chairs

Ancient Scripture

1994–97   Dennis L. Largey

1997–2000   Rex C. Reeve Jr.

2000–2002   Terry B. Ball

2002–4   Ray L. Huntington

2004–6   Dennis L. Largey

2006–7   David M. Whitchurch

2007–   Camille Fronk Olsen

Church History and Doctrine

1994–97   H. Dean Garrett

1997–2004   Arnold K. Garr

2004–6   Dennis A. Wright

2006–   John P. Livingstone

Ancient Studies Institute Directors

"Institute" dropped from the title when this area came under the Religious Studies Center in 1977

1973–77   Hugh Nibley

            Douglas Phillips (associate director)

1977–82   S. Kent Brown

1978–79   Thomas Mackay (interim director)

1982–97   C. Wilfred Griggs

1997–2006   S. Kent Brown

Religious Studies Center Publications Directors

1985–87   S. Kent Brown

1987–94   Charles D. Tate Jr.

1994–2001   Kent P. Jackson

2001–4   Richard D. Draper

2004–   Richard Neitzel Holzapfel

Richard L. Evans Chairs of Religious Understanding

Title changed from the Richard L. Evans Chair of Christian Understanding in 1994

1972–94	Truman G. Madsen
1994–98	David Paulsen
1996–99	Darwin L. Thomas
1998–2001	Larry C. Porter
1998–2005	Roger R. Keller
2001–5	Robert L. Millet
2005–	Fred E. Woods
2005–8	Paul Y. Hoskisson
2008–	James E. Faulconer

Appendix C

Full-Time Religious Education Faculty

Reasons for Leaving

D   Died

G   Called as a General Authority

L   Left BYU for other employment

R   Retired

T   Transferred to other university department or assignment

	Name	*Years on the Faculty*	
1.	Guy C. Wilson	1930–41	R
2.	Sidney B. Sperry	1932–69	R
3.	Russell R. Swensen	1933–47	T
4.	Wesley P. Lloyd	1938–48	T

5.	J. Wyley Sessions	1939–47	R			
6.	Hugh B. Brown	1946–49	L			
7.	Hugh Nibley	1946–75	R			
8.	William E. Berrett	1948–54	T	1971–73	R	
9.	Alma P. Burton	1948–54	L	1970–78	R	
10.	Roy W. Doxey	1948–74	R			
11.	Reid E. Bankhead	1949–85	R			
12.	Robert C. Patch	1949–54	L	1959–86	R	
13.	Eldin Ricks	1949–81	R			
14.	James R. Clark	1950–75	R			
15.	David H. Yarn Jr.	1950–73	T			
16.	B. West Belnap	1951–67	D			
17.	Glenn L. Pearson	1951–74	L			
18.	Ellis T. Rasmussen	1951–81	R			
19.	Chauncey C. Riddle	1952–69	T			
20.	Ivan J. Barrett	1953–75	R			
21.	Howard H. Barron	1953–85	R			
22.	Russell R. Rich	1953–77	R			
23.	Anthony I. Bentley	1954–73	R			
24.	J. Orval Ellsworth	1954–59	R			
25.	Gustive O. Larson	1954–67	R			
26.	Richard L. Anderson	1955–97	R			
27.	Hyrum L. Andrus	1955–75	T			
28.	Daniel H. Ludlow	1955–71	L			
29.	Lewis M. Rogers	1955–60	L			
30.	G. Byron Done	1956–72	R			
31.	H. Alvah Fitzgerald	1956–60	R			

32.	A. Burt Horsley	1956–84	R		
33.	Rodney Turner	1956–88	R		
34.	Truman G. Madsen	1957–73	T		
35.	Dale C. Tingey	1957–58	L		
36.	Keith H. Meservy	1958–90	R		
37.	F. Kent Nielsen	1958–66	T		
38.	Merlin L. Shaw	1959–63	D		
39.	Milton V. Backman Jr.	1960–91	R		
40.	Richard L. Bushman	1960–61	T		
41.	Richard O. Cowan	1961–			
42.	Spencer J. Palmer	1962–92	R		
43.	Wilson K. Andersen	1962–86	R		
44.	Paul E. Felt	1962–64	T	1974–81	R
45.	James B. Allen	1963–64	T		
46.	LaMar C. Berrett	1963–91	R		
47.	Walter D. Bowen	1964–95	R		
48.	Robert E. Parsons	1964–91	R		
49.	Melvin J. Petersen	1964–86	R		
50.	H. Donl Peterson	1964–93	R		
51.	J. Grant Stevenson	1964–90	R		
52.	Leon R. Hartshorn	1965–97	R		
53.	Paul R. Cheesman	1966–86	R		
54.	Alan D. Cook	1966–78	D		
55.	John P. Fugal	1966–86	R		
56.	James R. Harris	1966–87	R		
57.	Monte S. Nyman	1966–96	R		
58.	V. Ben Bloxham	1967–78	T		

59.	Jay W. Butler	1967–74	R		
60.	W. Cleon Skousen	1967–78	R		
61.	C. Terry Warner	1967–71	T		
62.	William E. Fort	1968–72	R		
63.	LaMar E. Garrard	1969–92	R		
64.	Hal L. Taylor	1969–83	R		
65.	George W. Pace	1970–93	R		
66.	Larry C. Porter	1970–2001	R		
67.	Dennis F. Rasmussen	1970–73	T		
68.	Noel B. Reynolds	1970–73	T		
69.	L. Grant Shields	1970–87	R		
70.	A. Gary Anderson	1971–94	R		
71.	S. Kent Brown	1971–2006	T		
72.	Robert J. Matthews	1971–92	R		
73.	Curtis E. Ledbetter	1972–83	R		
74.	Victor L. Ludlow	1972–			
75.	Leaun G. Otten	1972–95	R		
76.	C. Wilfred Griggs	1972–			
77.	Donald Q. Cannon	1973–2007	R		
78.	Jeffrey R. Holland	1974–76	L	1979–85	G
79.	George D. Durrant	1975–77	L	1989–94	L
80.	Keith W. Perkins	1975–99	R		
81.	James R. Moss	1976–88	L		
82.	Joseph F. McConkie	1977–2006	R		
83.	Reed A. Benson	1978–2003	R		
84.	James R. Christianson	1978–89	D		
85.	C. Max Caldwell	1978–92	G		

86.	Larry E. Dahl	1978–99	T
87.	Roger W. Gull	1978–86	R
88.	Clark V. Johnson	1979–2002	R
89.	John M. Lundquist	1979–85	L
90.	Kent P. Jackson	1980–	
91.	Paul Y. Hoskisson	1981–	
92.	Rex C. Reeve Jr.	1981–2003	R
93.	Susan Easton Black	1981–	
94.	George A. Horton Jr.	1983–92	R
95.	Robert L. Millet	1983–	
96.	Alan K. Parrish	1984–	
97.	Paul H. Peterson	1984–2007	R
98.	H. Dean Garrett	1985–2006	R
99.	D. Kelly Ogden	1986–	
100.	Stephen E. Robinson	1986–	
101.	S. Michael Wilcox	1986–90	L
102.	E. Dale LeBaron	1986–2001	R
103.	Bruce A. Van Orden	1986–2004	R
104.	Dennis L. Largey	1986–	
105.	John M. Madsen	1987–92	G
106.	David R. Seely	1987–	
107.	Brent L. Top	1987–	
108.	Dong Sull Choi	1987–	
109.	Richard D. Draper	1988–	
110.	Spencer J. Condie	1988–89	G
111.	Charles D. Tate Jr.	1988–94	R
112.	Roger R. Keller	1989–	

113.	M. Catherine Thomas	1989–92	L	1994–96	L
114.	Douglas E. Brinley	1990–2008	R		
115.	Raymond S. Wright III	1990–2003	R		
116.	Arnold K. Garr	1991–			
117.	Byron R. Merrill	1991–			
118.	Vern D. Sommerfeldt	1991–			
119.	Kip Sperry	1991–			
120.	Clyde J. Williams	1991–			
121.	Terry B. Ball	1992–			
122.	Jerome M. Perkins	1992–			
123.	Andrew C. Skinner	1992–			
124.	James A. Toronto	1992–2000	T		
125.	David F. Boone	1993–			
126.	Randy L. Bott	1993–			
127.	Lawrence R. Flake	1993–			
128.	Camille Fronk Olson	1993–			
129.	Richard Neitzel Holzapfel	1993–			
130.	Daniel K Judd	1993–			
131.	Todd B. Parker	1993–			
132.	Dana M. Pike	1993–			
133.	Guy L. Dorius	1994–			
134.	Stanley A. Johnson	1994–			
135.	Alexander L. Baugh	1995–			
136.	Ray L. Huntington	1995–			
137.	Craig J. Ostler	1995–			
138.	Gaye Strathearn	1995–			
139.	Keith J. Wilson	1995–			

140.	Dennis A. Wright	1995–	
141.	Robert C. Freeman	1996–	
142.	Andrew H. Hedges	1996–	
143.	Michael D. Rhodes	1996–	
144.	Matthew O. Richardson	1996–	
145.	Cynthia Doxey	1997–2008	L
146.	Maren Mauretsen	1997–99	R
147.	Lloyd D. Newell	1997–	
148.	Mary Jane Woodger	1997–	
149.	Richard E. Bennett	1998–	
150.	John P. Livingstone	1998–	
151.	W. Jeffrey Marsh	1998–	
152.	David M. Whitchurch	1998–	
153.	Fred E. Woods	1998–	
154.	Brian M. Hauglid	1999–	
155.	Frank F. Judd Jr.	1999–	
156.	Craig K. Manscill	1999–	
157.	John B. Stohlton	1999–	
158.	Terry L. Szink	1999–	
159.	Thomas A. Wayment	2000–	
160.	Kent R. Brooks	2001–	
161.	Jeffrey R. Chadwick	2001–	
162.	Steven C. Harper	2002–	
163.	Paul C. Warner	2002–5	R
164.	Eric D. Huntsman	2003–	
165.	Roger P. Minert	2003–	
166.	Charles Swift	2003–	

167.	J. Spencer Fluhman	2004–
168.	Alonzo L. Gaskill	2005–
169.	Scott C. Esplin	2006–
170.	Jared W. Ludlow	2006–
171.	Kerry M. Muhlestein	2006–
172.	Reid L. Neilson	2006–
173.	Michael A. Goodman	2007–
174.	Daniel Belnap	2007–
175.	Kenneth L. Alford	2008–

Following the creation of the Joseph Fielding Smith Institute of Church History, five members of that institute were assigned to Religious Education at different times for their academic affiliation:

Ronald K. Esplin

Richard L. Jensen

Dean C. Jessee

Jill Mulvay Derr

William G. Hartley